Impact English

MIKE GOULD, KIM RICHARDSON, MARY GREEN & JOHN MANNION

Key Stage 3 – Year 7 • Student Book 3

Contents

① A horror story

Aims

- ◗ Read a short story
- ◗ Learn how to skim and scan a text (R1, R2)
- ◗ Learn about prepositional phrases (S2)
- ◗ Learn that a text type can contain elements of other text types
- ◗ Learn about story endings (Wr5)

This story comes from *More Horowitz Horror* by Anthony Horowitz. When you come to the end, *don't do what the story asks you to do – yet!* You will follow this up later.

THE SHORTEST HORROR STORY EVER WRITTEN

I want to tell you how this story got included in this book.

About a week before the book was published, I broke into the offices of Orchard Books which are located in a rather grubby street near Liverpool Street Station. Maybe you haven't noticed but the book
5   you are holding at this very minute was published by Orchard and I wanted to get my hands on it because, you see, I'd had an idea.

Generally speaking, publishers are stupid lazy people. Orchard Books have about twenty people working for them but not one of them noticed that a window had been forced open in the
10 middle of the night and that someone had added a couple of pages to the collection of horror stories that was sitting by the computer, waiting to be sent to the printers. I had brought these pages with me, you see, because I wanted to

add my own message to the book. Nobody noticed and nobody cared and if you are reading this then I'm afraid my plan has worked and you are about to discover the meaning of true horror. Get ready – because here it comes.

Twelve years ago I desperately wanted to be a writer and so I wrote a horror story (based on my own experiences) which was rejected by every publisher in London because, they claimed, it wasn't frightening enough! Of course, none of them had the faintest idea what horror really meant because they had never actually committed a murder whereas I, my dear reader, had committed several.

My Uncle Frederick was my first victim, followed by my next-door neighbour (an unpleasant little man with a moustache and a smelly cat), two total strangers, an actor who once had a bit part in EastEnders and a Jehovah's Witness who happened to knock at my door while I was cooking lunch. Unfortunately, my adventures came to an end when a dim-witted policeman stopped my car just as I was disposing of the last body and I was arrested and sent to a lunatic asylum for life. Recently, however, I escaped and it was after that that I had the wonderful idea which you are reading about at this very moment and which can be summarised in three simple stages. Drop into the offices of one of those smarmy publishers in London and slip a couple of pages into somebody else's book (with many apologies to Anthony Horowitz, whoever he may be). Exit quietly and stay in hiding until the book is published. Return only when the book is in the shops and then wait in the background, until some poor fool buys it and follow that person home…

Yes, dear reader, at this very moment I could be sitting outside your home or your school or wherever you happen to be and if by any chance you are the one I've chosen, I'm afraid you're about to learn a lesson about horror that I know you'd prefer to miss. Orchard Books are also going to wish that they'd published me all those years ago, especially when they start losing readers in particularly nasty ways, one by one. Understanding will come – but I'm afraid you're going to have to read this whole story again.

Start at the beginning. Only this time look carefully at the first word of each sentence. Or to be more precise, the first letter of each first word. Now, at last, I hope you can see quite how gloriously, hideously mad I really am – although for you, perhaps, it may already be too late.

Key Reading

> ## Narrative texts
>
> This text is a story or **narrative**. The **purpose** of a narrative is to entertain us.
>
> The main feature of a narrative text is:
>
> - It has a structure that includes an **introduction**, a **complication**, a **crisis** (where the plot comes to a high point) and a **resolution** (when things are sorted out).

The Shortest Horror Story Ever Written follows this structure – up to a point!

- **Introduction:** We find out how the story got into the book.

- **Complication:** The 'writer' is a murderer seeking revenge.

1 Do you think there is a crisis in the narrative? If there is, where does it come?

2 In what way is the resolution in this story different from a conventional narrative?

3 Why is this line comical: '(with many apologies to Anthony Horowitz, whoever he may be)'?

4 The writer opens the story by saying to the reader, 'I want to tell you…' This makes us feel close to the writer. He seems to be speaking directly to us. The writer speaks to us at the beginning of one other paragraph. Find the paragraph and the words.

5 The writer shifts between the past and the present in the story. In the second sentence he writes, 'About a week *before*…'. This time connective refers to the past.

    a) Identify a time connective that refers to the present.

    b) In what way does the narrative also refer to the future? Find evidence in the last two paragraphs.

Purpose

 6 Think of more than one reason why the author wrote this story. Discuss what you think is the main reason.

Reading for meaning

To read the message in the story you will need to **scan** the text. Scanning a text is a good way to get information quickly. It means you skip words to find what you are looking for.

R2 **7** Scan the story and work out the message, following the instructions given in the last paragraph. Write down the first letter of each sentence as you go and then read the message.

Exploring further: Skimming

We **skim** a text when we read it quickly for the first time. This tells us what the text is roughly about and how it is told. For example, we often skim the blurb on the back of a book, to get a quick idea of what the book is about. The following comes from the blurb on *More Horowitz Horror*.

> Here are eight nerve-tinglingly nightmarish stories
> to make your skin crawl
> and the blood freeze in your veins.
>
> Unmasking the strange, the macabre and the downright
> diabolical, these stories will make you think...they'll make you
> shiver...they'll make you afraid.

R1 **8 a)** Write three short blurbs, choosing from the following types or genres.

● Horror ● Animal ● Detective ● Historical ● Non-fiction

Ensure that your blurbs are written in different styles to suit the genre, like the example above. Do not mention the genre by name; the reader should be able to guess.

 b) Give your blurb to a partner to skim and guess what genre it is.

Focus on: Story endings

The Shortest Horror Story Ever Written has a **twist** or surprise at the end. So does the following example.

The End

Not quite...

As you see, a story with a twist can mean that the story has not ended.

This is also true of **cliffhangers**. These often come at the end of a chapter in a book. They create tension or suspense. For example:

All at once there was a clattering of hooves. A ghost-rider with a long ragged cloak appeared. He grasped a flaming torch in his hand. Then another came and another and another. They swung the torches above their heads. They hurled them into the crowd. As the people fled, a noise like the sound of thunder came from behind the hill. Slowly, a giant shadow loomed and then something appeared. Something more dreadful than anything the people had seen before.

In **descriptions** like this, it is a good idea to vary the sentences. This makes the writing more interesting and it keeps the reader's attention.

> He grasped a flaming torch in his hand.

We could change this sentence round:

> In his hand he grasped a flaming torch.

Wr5

9 Choose from one of the following options:

    a) Use the illustrations and captions on page 8 to write a story ending with a twist, of approximately 75 words.

    b) Extend the cliffhanger example on page 8 by adding approximately 75 words. You should end with a more exciting cliffhanger.

    Remember to vary your sentences to keep your writing interesting.

Exploring further: Prepositional phrases

Prepositions tell us where things are and when or where things are happening. For example: 'at', 'into', 'before', 'after', 'about', 'around'.

We sometimes use the same preposition in more than one way.
- He arrived *around* midnight. (Time: *when* he arrived.)
- He tied the string *around* the parcel. (Place: *where* he tied the string.)

A **prepositional phrase** connects two nouns in a sentence.

For example, *around* connects 'He' and 'midnight'.

S2

10 a) Write down the three prepositional phrases in the cliffhanger example on page 8.

    b) Next to each of them, note down what kind of prepositional phrase they are.

Key Writing

11 Write a short horror story with a twist. You could base it on one of the following themes (or your own idea):

- mistaken identity (for example, involving identical twins)
- something priceless that turns out to be worthless
- an outsider returns to seek revenge
- a house that has unearthly powers.

Remember:

- vary your sentences
- use some prepositional phrases
- include powerful description.

You might like to start like this:

I pushed open the great oak door. It creaked. I stopped and listened. There were no voices. I slipped out and walked straight towards the iron gates. I could hear my feet crunching on the gravel. Eight, nine, ten, I was almost there...

② Big fears

- Read the poem, *Big Fears*
- Learn what 'repetition' means (R14)
- Learn about creating images and metaphors (Wr8)
- Learn about a range of sound effects (Wr8)
- Write a poem

We all have our own fears and worries. At night they seem to grow. Read this poem by John Rice and find out what Sian, Matthew and Karen worry about.

Big Fears

Twenty-five feet above Sian's house
hangs a thick wire cable
that droops and sags between two
electricity pylons.
5 A notice says it carries 40,000 volts
from one metallic scarecrow to the next,
Then on to the next and the next
right across the countryside to the city.
The cable sways above Sian's council house
10 making her radio crackle and sometimes
making her television go on the blink.

If it's a very windy night
Sian gets frightened because she
thinks the cable might snap,
15 fall onto the roof and electrocute
everyone as they sleep.

This is Sian's Big Fear.

Outside Matthew's bedroom there
is a tall tree. Taller than the house.
20 In summer it is heavy with huge leaves.
In winter it stands lonely as a morning moon.

On a windy night, Matthew worries
that the tree might be blown down
and crash through his bedroom window.
25 It would certainly kill him and his cat
if it wasn't in its own cardboard box.

This is Matthew's Big Fear.

Outside Karen's bedroom there's nothing
but a pleasant view, meadows, hedges, sheep
30 and some distant gentle hills.
There's nothing sinister, nothing to worry about.

But in the dark Karen thinks
the darting shapes on the ceiling
are really the shadows of a ghost's
35 great cold hands and that the night noises
made by the water pipes are the
screeches and groans of attic skeletons.

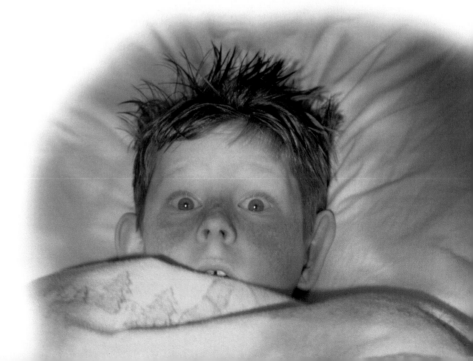

Key Reading

Poetry

This text is a **poem**. Its **purpose** is to explore feelings and ideas.

A poem is made up of **images**, **rhythm** and **form**.
- The **images** are the pictures made by the words.
- The **rhythm** is like the beat in music.
- The **form** is the framework or pattern of the poem. Poems are written in **lines** not sentences.

Poems can be written in different styles:
- Some poems **rhyme**, for example, doom/gloom/tomb.
- Some poems are **free verse**. They have lines of different lengths with different rhythms. (Some free verse contains rhyme.)

To work out the rhythm of *Big Fears*, listen to those parts of words (**syllables**) that are stressed. For example, '*twen*-ty' has two syllables. We stress the syllable '*twen*-'; the other syllable ('-ty') is unstressed.

1 a) Gently tap out the rhythm of this line from *Big Fears*.

> Twenty-five feet above Sian's house
> hangs a thick wire cable
> that droops and sags between two
> electricity pylons.

b) Do the lines have the same rhythm?

2 Referring to the styles listed above, what style of poem do you think *Big Fears* is and why?

Image and metaphor

Images appeal to the reader's senses. Most images appeal to the sense of sight, but they can also appeal to the senses of sound, touch, taste and smell.

A **metaphor** is an image that presents one thing as another. For example, thunder might be called 'the god of war'.

3 a) In the first verse of *Big Fears*, identify:

● an image that appeals to the reader's sense of sound

● a metaphor.

b) In the last verse of the poem, find an image that appeals to:

● the reader's sense of sound

● one other sense apart from sight.

Purpose

Big Fears explores different feelings and ideas about fear.

4 a) Reread the poem and identify the fears of Sian, Matthew and Karen.

Wr3

b) Write a short paragraph about the kinds of fear explored in the poem. Consider in what way Karen's fear is different from Sian's and Matthew's, using evidence from the poem.

Reading for meaning

When writing poetry in lines, words that are used in sentences are sometimes dropped. This can add to the impact of a poem. For example:

> Outside Matthew's bedroom there is a tall tree. Taller than the house.

If these lines are written as full sentences, a pronoun and a verb are added:

> Outside Matthew's bedroom there is a tall tree. *It is* taller than the house.

Without 'It is', the words, '…tall tree. Taller…' are closer together. This stresses the height of the tree.

The lines also read differently – the reader's voice rises and falls more in the lines than in the sentences. This is called **cadence**. For example, more stress is put on the word '*Taller*' in the lines. Again, this draws attention to the height of the tree.

R14

5 Read the two lines and the two full sentences again, listening to the difference in your voice.

6 a) Now read the sentence below and turn it into lines:

> At night when I hear the tap, tap, tap of the branch on the window I dream of ghosts.

b) Arrange the lines to make a different form. Experiment with several ideas. Emphasise the movement and sound of the branch in your new form.

c) Add a few more lines developing the image of the ghost. Think about the kinds of feelings you are trying to create. (You may wish to refer to the first and last verses of *Big Fears*.)

Exploring further: Sound effects

Like music, poetry creates a variety of sound effects. These reinforce the mood and meaning of the poem.

You have seen how more stress is placed on the word '*Taller*' in the lines than in the sentence. In addition, the long 'all' sound helps to reinforce the height of the tree:

'there is a tall tree.

*Tall*er than the house.'

Alliteration

When words near each other begin with the same sound, it is called **alliteration**. The use of the letter 't' above is an example of alliteration.

7 a) What alliteration is used in the following lines?

> In summer it is heavy with huge leaves.
> In winter it stands lonely as a morning moon.

b) What does the alliteration suggest the tree is like?

Wr8

c) Write two lines using alliteration that describe the tree in spring and autumn. Each line should create an image.

Exploring further: Consonance

This is another sound effect. It occurs when the end or inner consonants of words are repeated. For example, 'se**nd** the wild wi**nd**.' (This is called half-rhyme when rhymed at the end of lines.)

8 Find an example of consonance in the following lines:

…the tree might be blown down
and crash through his bedroom window.
It would certainly kill him and his cat
if it wasn't in its own cardboard box.

Poets often create these effects without realising it. Listen to the sound of your own poems when you are writing to see what effects are present.

Focus on: Repetition

Using repetition in a poem helps to give the poem **form**. It also helps to emphasise what the poem is about, as shown in this verse from *Big Fears*.

> If it's a very windy night
> Sian gets frightened because she
> thinks the cable might snap,
> fall onto the roof and electrocute
> everyone as they sleep.
>
> This is Sian's Big Fear.

This line is repeated in the poem

R14

9 a) What else in the last line emphasises that the poem is about fear?

b) Why do you think this line is set apart from the other lines?

c) The line could be written in another place in the poem. Where would that be? Why?

Key Writing

Wr8 **10** Imagine that you are a restless ghost, forever returning to a scene from your unhappy past. Write a poem about yourself.

Draw on the work you have done in this unit, adapting it to suit your poem. Experiment with your lines until you are satisfied.

Remember to include a range of features:

- a powerful setting
- varied line lengths
- a repeating line or lines that will remind the reader that you are constantly returning to the same place
- powerful images
- sound effects
- anything else you think reinforces the meaning of the poem.

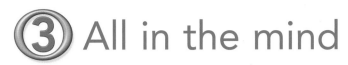

③ All in the mind

Aims

▶ Read and present an argument text

▶ Understand words in context (W16)

▶ Use paragraphs to follow the main points (R7)

▶ Record points and supporting evidence in a flow chart (Wr2)

▶ Adopt a range of roles in discussion and contribute by exploring and questioning (S&L11, S&L14)

Do ghosts really exist? Read the following article from a BBC web page and find out!

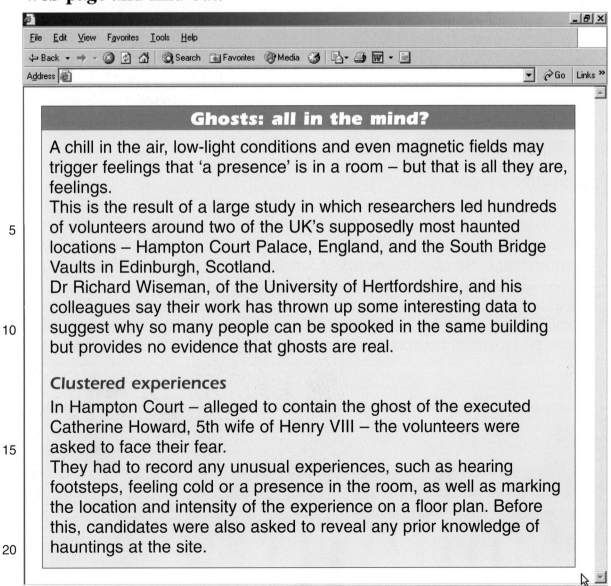

Ghosts: all in the mind?

A chill in the air, low-light conditions and even magnetic fields may trigger feelings that 'a presence' is in a room – but that is all they are, feelings.

5 This is the result of a large study in which researchers led hundreds of volunteers around two of the UK's supposedly most haunted locations – Hampton Court Palace, England, and the South Bridge Vaults in Edinburgh, Scotland.

Dr Richard Wiseman, of the University of Hertfordshire, and his colleagues say their work has thrown up some interesting data to 10 suggest why so many people can be spooked in the same building but provides no evidence that ghosts are real.

Clustered experiences

In Hampton Court – alleged to contain the ghost of the executed Catherine Howard, 5th wife of Henry VIII – the volunteers were 15 asked to face their fear.

They had to record any unusual experiences, such as hearing footsteps, feeling cold or a presence in the room, as well as marking the location and intensity of the experience on a floor plan. Before this, candidates were also asked to reveal any prior knowledge of 20 hauntings at the site.

The researchers then examined the distribution of unusual experiences. In a 'normal' setting, you would expect the ghostly encounters to be evenly spaced, but in classic haunting, they would be clustered around certain places.

25 The results were striking: participants did record a higher number of unusual experiences in the most classically haunted places of Hampton Court, areas such as the Georgian rooms and the Haunted Gallery. And in the Edinburgh vaults, the results were the same – the vaults considered most haunted were the locations where the most unusual encounters occurred during the study.

Environmental cues

30 The researchers interpret this as evidence that the hauntings are a real phenomenon because they are concentrated in specific places over time. Indeed, it is known for people from different cultures to consistently report similar experiences over perhaps hundreds of years.

"Hauntings exist, in the sense that places exist where people reliably have

35 unusual experiences," Dr Richard Wiseman told BBC News Online. "The existence of ghosts is a way of explaining these experiences."

But are the ghosts real? Dr Wiseman and his colleagues are not so sure. They claim, somewhat paradoxically, that the hauntings exist but the ghosts do not.

"People do have consistent experiences in consistent places, but I think that

40 this is driven by visual factors mainly, and perhaps some other environmental cues," he said.

Sensitive people

Making detailed measurements at each place, such as temperature, light intensity and room space, Dr Wiseman thinks that people are responding

45 unconsciously to environmental cues and the general 'spookiness' of their surroundings. He cites examples of mediums successfully indicating haunted areas of buildings with no prior knowledge of them.

Spiritualists interpret this as evidence that the ghosts are there, but another explanation is that the mediums are simply more sensitive to the environmental

50 cues that result in haunted feelings – not sensitivity to the ghosts themselves.

Key Reading

Argument texts

This text is a report that contains an **argument**. The **purpose** of an argument is to present a point of view so that others will accept it.

The main features of an argument text are:

● It usually has an **opening statement** that introduces the argument.

● It presents the argument clearly, making **points** one at a time.

● It uses **evidence** to back up points, for example, 'Dr Richard Wiseman…and his colleagues…say…'

● It uses **connectives** that help link one idea with another, for example, 'It suggests why…*but*…'

● It is told mainly in the **present tense**, for example, '…that *is* all they are…'.

● It may use other tenses, for example, 'They *had* to record…' (past tense).

1 There are two main tenses used in the text. Look again at paragraphs 3, 4, 7, 9 and 11, and decide what tenses these are written in or *mainly* written in.

Copy and complete the chart below to record your answers. In the last column, explain your decision. The first paragraph has already been done for you, as an example.

Paragraph	Tense	Explanation
3	Present	*The writer is telling us what Dr Wiseman and his colleagues think now.*

2 Look through your completed chart and then write a short paragraph to explain why the tenses are used at different points in the text. You could begin, 'The present tense is used when...'

3 a) In the first sentence there is a verb (called a modal) that tells us something *might* happen. What is it?

b) Which of the following verbs are modals?

- go
- is
- have
- could
- made
- may
- are
- run

Purpose

4 What does the argument in the article try to prove to the reader?

5 Where did this article first appear? How does this affect its purpose?

Reading for meaning

Vocabulary

W16 **6** Some of the vocabulary found in the article is challenging. To help you work out what the following words mean, replace each word with either option a) or option b) listed below. Write down your answers.

alleged (line 13)	a) supposed	b) sworn
clustered (line 23)	a) bunched	b) crushed
environmental cues (line 45)	a) signs of spirits	b) background signals
distribution (line 21)	a) spread	b) sprinkling
phenomenon (line 31)	a) miracle	b) occurrence
cites (line 46)	a) accuses	b) highlights
paradoxically (line 38)	a) uncertainly	b) illogically

Opening statements

In order to follow the argument, you need to understand:

● the points being made

● the evidence given.

It is a good idea to start by looking at the **opening statement**. We can ask some basic questions such as: What? Where? Who?

7 a) Look at the opening section and answer the second question in short notes.

Question	Answer
What is the argument?	Ghosts do not exist.
What is the evidence?	

b) Look over the section again and ask two questions of your own beginning:

● Where…? ● Who…?

c) Ask a partner to answer your questions. Remember, the opening section gives us an idea of what an argument text is about. Study it to ask basic questions.

The main points of an argument

The text can also help us to find the main points of an argument.

● Subheadings help us to find information.

● The first few words (or **topic sentence**) of a paragraph can give us clues.

Look at the following examples from the text:

> **Subheading:** 'Clustered experiences'
>
> **First few words of paragraphs (or topic sentence):**
>
> ● 'In Hampton Court…'
>
> ● 'They had to record…'

From this information, you can tell what these paragraphs are about:

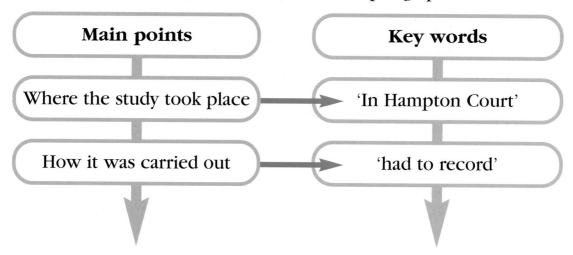

Main points	Key words
Where the study took place	→ 'In Hampton Court'
How it was carried out	→ 'had to record'

R7, Wr2

8 a) Find the first words or topic sentence of the other paragraphs under 'Clustered experiences' and decide what the main points are. Record them in a flow chart like the one shown above.

b) Then find the subheading 'Environmental cues' and do the same.

• •

Focus on: Presenting the evidence

Evidence is given to back up the main argument in the text: that ghosts do not exist. It is taken from Dr Wiseman's study at Hampton Court and the Edinburgh vaults.

9 a) Scan the text to find all the places where Dr Wiseman is mentioned. Note these down.

b) Add these to the flow chart to show where evidence is presented to support the argument.

10 Find the words used to give Dr Wiseman's results. For example, 'Dr Richard Wiseman…and his colleagues *say*…'; 'The researchers *interpret*…' Note down the words.

11 Scan the last paragraph for an example of evidence presented from another point of view.

Exploring further

12 Read the last two paragraphs again, under 'Sensitive people'. Copy out this chart and record notes under the headings.

What spiritualists think	What the researchers think	What I think

13 Write your point of view in two linking paragraphs. Refer to the evidence on both sides, using the chart above.

Key Speaking and Listening

14 a) Work in groups to present an argument that challenges Dr Wiseman's evidence. To do this you will need to study the evidence again. Check:
- what experiences the volunteers had in haunted places
- what the researchers said this meant
- whether this is proof that ghosts don't exist.

.11, S&L14

b) Discuss these points together and decide on the main points of your argument.
- Reinterpret some of the original evidence to support your argument.
- Use some of the language of argument, for example, 'some might say', 'others insist', 'researchers might claim'.
- Use some of the words you have learned, such as 'phenomenon' and 'environmental cues'.

Make notes or a flow chart to record your main points and the evidence for these.

c) Appoint a group member to act as spokesperson and report back to the class.

④ Unit 1 Assignment: The poet

Assessment Focuses

▶ **AF1** Write imaginative, interesting and thoughtful texts

▶ **AF7** Select appropriate and effective vocabulary

> **You:** are a poet.
> **Your task:** to write a poem about horror.

Stage 1

Most feelings can be compared to something concrete. For example, jealousy is sometimes called 'the green-eyed monster'. Below are some things to compare horror to:

● the red-eyed demon
● the sudden fever
● the icy chill.

Add more descriptions to the list. Use a thesaurus to help you.

Stage 2

Now take your descriptions from Stage 1 and create images.
For example, using **similes** you could create:

> Horror is *like* the red-eyed demon.
> As horrific *as* the red-eyed demon.

Using **metaphors**, replace 'horror' with:

> The red-eyed demon.

Use the images you create to develop your lines.
For example, start with a metaphor and add a simile:

> The *red-eyed* demon is *like* a shadow.

Or use more interesting verbs:

> The red-eyed demon, *skulking* like a shadow.

Find interesting verbs in a thesaurus. Try out different ideas.

Stage 3

Use the work you have done to write a free verse poem about horror. Experiment by arranging your lines in different ways. For example, you could change the line in the example above to:

> *Skulking* like a shadow, the red-eyed demon.

Or you could create a 'run-on' line:

> *Skulking in the shadows,* the red-eyed demon
> Creeps.

You could imagine yourself as 'horror':

> *I am* the red-eyed demon, skulking like a shadow.
> *I am…*

You could create form by repeating words or lines, and also break the repetition at some point in the poem.

You could also write a comic poem or 'spoof', where you exaggerate the horror.

Challenge

'Horror' (like 'jealousy') is an **abstract noun** (something we cannot see). In the poem you have written you personified 'horror'. **Personification** is a type of metaphor that makes an idea or an object seem like a person. Think of your own abstract nouns or choose from the following list, and write a series of verses:

● anger ● power ● ambition ● greed ● envy ● hate.

Think of different ways to connect the verses so that the whole poem deals with a range of abstract nouns. For example, you could link the verses using a word or a line.

Myths and legends

① The apples of the Hesperides

Aims

▶ Read a Greek myth

▶ Think about the purpose of myths and why they have remained popular (R20)

▶ Discover how a storyteller builds up a picture of the characters (R16)

▶ Learn why writers vary the length and structure of their sentences, and practise doing this yourself (S18)

This story comes from a book of Ancient Greek myths, retold by Geraldine McCaughrean. The Greek hero Heracles has superhuman strength. However, he has killed his family in a drunken frenzy caused by the goddess Hera. As a punishment, he becomes the slave of the spiteful King Eurystheus. Before he can be free, he has to complete twelve difficult and dangerous tasks for the king – the Labours of Heracles.

The Apples of the Hesperides

The twelfth and last of the king's commands was for Heracles to bring him the apples of the Hesperides. These magical fruit grew on a tree in a garden at the end of the world, and around that tree coiled a dragon which never slept.

5   Even Heracles, with all his courage and strength, quailed at the thought of fighting the dragon. So Heracles went to see a giant named Atlas.

Now Atlas was no ordinary giant, as big as a house. Atlas was the biggest man in the world, and towered above houses, trees, cliffs

10 and hills. He was so tall that the gods had given him the task of

holding up the sky and keeping the stars from falling. The sun scorched his neck and the new moon shaved his beard. And for thousands of years he had stood in the one spot.

15 "How can I go to the end of the world?" said Atlas, when Heracles asked him for the favour. "How can I go *anywhere*?"

"I could hold the sky for you while you were gone," suggested Heracles.

"Could you? Would you? Then I'll do it!" said Atlas.

20 So Heracles took the sky on his back – though it was the heaviest burden he had ever carried. Atlas stretched himself, then strode away towards the end of the world.

Fetching the apples was no hardship. But as the giant hurried back across the world, carrying the precious fruit, the thought of carrying that weight of sky again seemed less and less attractive.

25 His steps slowed. When at last he reached Heracles – poor, exhausted, bone-bent Heracles – Atlas exclaimed, "I've decided! I'm going to let *you* go on holding up the sky, and *I'll* deliver these apples to King Eurystheus."

There was a silence. Then Heracles grunted, "Fine. Thank you.

30 It's a great honour to be allowed to hold up heaven. But if you could just help me get a pad across my shoulders before you go…these stars do prickle…"

So Atlas took charge of the sky again – just while Heracles made a pad for his shoulders. He even gave Heracles the apples to

35 hold, because he needed both hands.

"Well, I'll be on my way now," said Heracles, juggling with the apples as he scurried away.

★   ★   ★   ★   ★   ★   ★   ★   ★   ★

After seven years, Heracles' hard labours came to an end, and he was free. But he was never free from his sorrow at taking

40 that first glass of wine: not until the day he died.

Being a man and not a god, he did die. But the gods did not forget him. They cut him out in stars and hung him in the sky, to rest from his labours for all time, among the singing planets.

Key Reading

Narrative texts

This text is a **narrative**. Its **purpose** is to tell a story.

The main features of a narrative text are:

● It has a structure that includes an **introduction**, a **complication**, a **crisis** (where everything comes to a high point) and a **resolution** (when things are sorted out).

● It has **characters** who the story is about. The reader often hears their words and thoughts.

● There is also a **narrator**, who tells the story. For example, 'Now Atlas was no ordinary giant' is the narrator telling us about the character Atlas.

● It uses **powerful words**. The narrative must be interesting to read or listen to, for example, 'poor, exhausted, bone-bent Heracles'.

● It is written in **chronological order**, using **time connectives** to show the sequence of events, for example, '*When* at last he reached Heracles…'

1 If you were making a cartoon version of the final labour of Heracles, and you only had four boxes to fill, what scene would you choose for your:
   a) introduction   **c)** crisis
   b) complication   **d)** resolution?

2 What scenes would you choose from the myth if you were telling the whole story of Heracles' life and death?

3 The story of the twelfth task ends by telling us what Heracles does and says once he has the apples. Add a sentence to tell the reader what Atlas's reaction is.

4 In the final line the narrator says that Heracles 'scurried away'. How and why is this better than saying that Heracles 'ran away'?

5 'The sun scorched his neck and the new moon shaved his beard' (lines 11–12). What makes this an effective description?

6 The writing is also very plain at times, for example, 'So Heracles went to see a giant named Atlas' (line 6). Can you explain why myths are often written in this way?

7 The last section leaps forward in time.

a) How does the writer indicate this?

b) Why does she also refer back to the beginning of Heracles' story?

• •

Purpose

The purpose of a narrative is to entertain us by telling a good story. Myths make good stories for several reasons:

● They are often action-packed.

● The characters are larger than life, such as gods, heroes and monsters.

R20

8 What features of *The Apples of the Hesperides* make it an entertaining myth? Think about the characters as well as the story.

9 Myths have another purpose. They say important things about the world and the people in it. In *The Apples of the Hesperides*, Heracles has to complete a difficult and dangerous task.

a) What qualities does he show in the way he manages to complete the task?

b) Think of a difficult task that you managed to complete. What qualities did you show?

10 Heroes in myths often have to complete many dangerous tasks or tests. Sometimes this involves a long journey.

a) Note down some other heroes who have to carry out dangerous tasks. Think about heroes from myths, novels, films or comics.

b) Why do you think overcoming difficulty to become a hero or heroine is such a popular theme for a narrative?

Reading for meaning

A storyteller builds up a picture of the characters in three main ways:

- By describing what the characters do.
- By telling us what the characters say.
- By telling us how the characters look or feel.

11 Analyse how the writer builds up a picture of Atlas in the story. Draw up and complete a chart like the one below.

Information about Atlas	Example from the text	How this builds up a picture of Atlas
What Atlas does	Atlas has the task of 'holding up the sky and keeping the stars from falling' (line 11).	This shows how incredibly strong Atlas must be.
What Atlas says		
What Atlas looks like		

12 a) Now draw up a similar table for Heracles.

b) The writer plays down Heracles' great strength in this episode. Why does she do this? Is this successful?

Exploring further: Punctuation

The **dash** can be used to indicate a pause (like a comma), an afterthought, or to separate off a phrase or clause (like using brackets).

13 Find an example of each use of a dash in the story.

The three-dot **ellipsis** (…) punctuates text in two main ways:

- It shows that one or more words have been missed out of a quotation, for example: *The longest sentence in the extract is 'But as the giant…less and less attractive.'*
- It shows an unfinished sentence or thought, for example: *'But what would you do? I mean…' Max took a deep breath and looked out of the window.*

14 The writer has used ellipsis twice in paragraph 9. What effect does this have?

• •

Focus on: Sentence structure

Good storytellers vary the length of their sentences to keep the reader interested.

15 Look at the sentences below and make notes on how the writer uses variety in sentence length to create an effect. Use the terms 'contrast', 'separate clauses' and 'simple sentence' in your notes. The first note has been done for you as an example.

> A short, clear, simple sentence to start the paragraph

> Fetching the apples was no hardship. But as the giant hurried back across the world, carrying the precious fruit, the thought of carrying that weight of sky again seemed less and less attractive. His steps slowed.

S18

16 a) Rewrite the second sentence above as three shorter sentences and compare the effect.

b) Find another complex sentence in the story and explain why it has been used.

c) There are many compound sentences linking clauses with 'and' in the first half of the story. Identify these and explain why they are particularly common in a myth or traditional tale.

Grammar for reading

A **simple sentence** contains just one main clause, for example, 'His steps slowed.' A **compound sentence** contains two or more main clauses joined by connectives such as 'and', 'but', 'for', 'or', 'yet' or 'so', for example, 'His steps slowed and then he stopped'. A **complex sentence** contains a main clause and one or more subordinate clauses which do not make sense on their own, for example, 'His steps slowed because he was tired.'

Key Writing

17 Now write two or three short paragraphs describing Heracles' first task:
- He is sent to face a fierce lion.
- He kills the lion with his bare hands.
- From that point on he wears the lion's skin.
- This is a sign of his success and his strength.

Remember:
- Include descriptions of how Heracles looks and feels and what he says.
- Vary the length and type of your sentences to make your descriptions more interesting and dramatic.
- Include some time connectives to make the sequence of events clear.

You might start like this:
Now that Heracles was his slave, King Eurystheus set him his first task.

The science of Superman

Aims

▶ Read a text explaining why Superman is so strong

▶ Look at how explanation texts are written and organised (S13c)

▶ Understand words in context (W14)

▶ Learn about the links between cause and effect and how they are highlighted

▶ Write your own short explanation (Wr12)

The following text comes from a BBC web page.

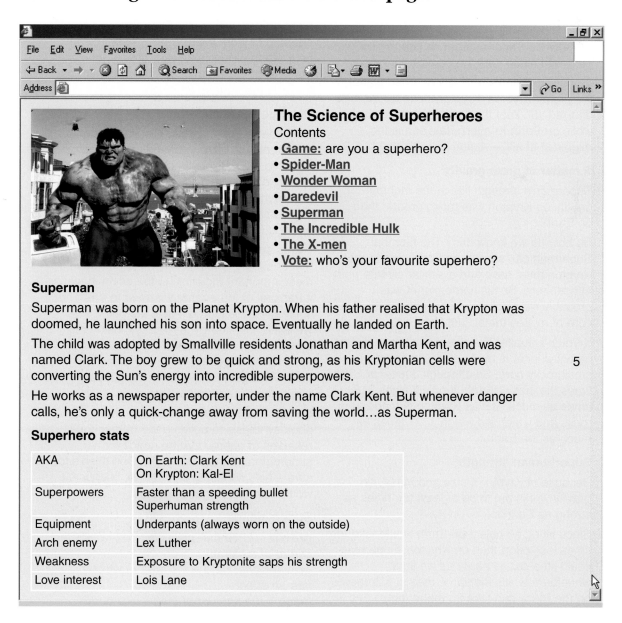

The Science of Superheroes
Contents
• **Game:** are you a superhero?
• **Spider-Man**
• **Wonder Woman**
• **Daredevil**
• **Superman**
• **The Incredible Hulk**
• **The X-men**
• **Vote:** who's your favourite superhero?

Superman

Superman was born on the Planet Krypton. When his father realised that Krypton was doomed, he launched his son into space. Eventually he landed on Earth.

The child was adopted by Smallville residents Jonathan and Martha Kent, and was named Clark. The boy grew to be quick and strong, as his Kryptonian cells were converting the Sun's energy into incredible superpowers.   5

He works as a newspaper reporter, under the name Clark Kent. But whenever danger calls, he's only a quick-change away from saving the world…as Superman.

Superhero stats

AKA	On Earth: Clark Kent On Krypton: Kal-El
Superpowers	Faster than a speeding bullet Superhuman strength
Equipment	Underpants (always worn on the outside)
Arch enemy	Lex Luther
Weakness	Exposure to Kryptonite saps his strength
Love interest	Lois Lane

Super-strength

10 So how did Superman get so strong? Let's start with clues from the comic:

'Superman comes from a long-dead planet, the planet Krypton. Krypton's Jupiter-like size and red sun kept the Kryptonian race weak, 15 while on Earth Krypton's last son is the mightiest of all!' – *Action Comics* no.14

A matter of great gravity

Superman's strength lies in the fact that the gravity on Krypton was much greater than 20 on Earth.

So how do we know this? The fact that Superman can survive on Earth means that Krypton must have had a similar climate and atmosphere. So his home planet was 25 probably made of rocks and water, with a core of molten metal, just like Earth.

Krypton's Jupiter-like size would make it very heavy. Jupiter is made of gas, with only a small rocky core. So although Jupiter is 1321 30 times the size of Earth, it only weighs 318 times as much. But as Krypton is made from rocks and water, it'd weigh 1321 times as much as the Earth.

Superhuman strength

35 Because of Krypton's size and mass, its gravity works out to be at least ten times as strong as Earth's.

Since lifting an object on Earth would take ten times less effort than on Krypton, Superman 40 could lift a car as easily as we lift a wheelbarrow. It's the same reason astronauts on the Moon can take 25 metre jumps and lift huge objects with ease. Their muscles have adapted to work in the Earth's gravitational field. So the Moon's weaker gravity (one sixth 45 the strength of Earth's) doesn't pull them back towards the surface as much.

Solar-powered superhero

How does Superman trap the Sun's energy? While animals have to eat plants (or each 50 other) to survive, plants can harvest their energy directly from the Sun's light by photosynthesis. This is a chemical reaction that converts carbon dioxide and water into glucose (a type of sugar) and oxygen. 55

Plants are full of a chemical called chlorophyll that speeds this reaction up. It is perhaps the most important molecule in the world, because it traps all of the energy we need to live. The solar energy is stored inside the plant; when 60 we eat it, this energy is released inside our bodies. All of our coal and oil reserves were once made of plants. This means that the energy we get from petrol to run our cars originally came from the Sun. 65

So perhaps Superman is using some form of photosynthesis to build up the tremendous reserves of energy that he needs for his superhuman feats of strength. One thing's for sure – he's not using chlorophyll, because it 70 would turn him bright green!

Superscience

gravity – *force that pulls objects towards the centre of a planet*
gravitational field – *the area in which gravity has an effect* 75
mass – *the amount of matter in a body*

Key Reading

Explanation texts

This text is (mainly) an **explanation**. Its **purpose** is to help someone understand how something works or why something has happened.

The main features of an explanation text are:

● It includes a series of **clear and logical steps**, for example: '*Let's start with* clues from the comic' highlights the first step.

● It uses **causal language** which shows how one thing causes another, for example, '*Because* of Krypton's size and mass, its gravity works out to be at least ten times as strong as Earth's.'

● It uses **precise vocabulary** and technical terms may be explained in a glossary, for example, 'plants can harvest their energy directly from the Sun's light by *photosynthesis*.'

● It is written in the **present tense** when explaining how or why something is now, for example, 'How *does* Superman trap the Sun's energy?'

S13c

1 One section of the website has been annotated below to show examples of all of these features. Make a note of examples of these features in the next section of the website ('Solar-powered superhero').

causal language, signalled by 'because'

causal language, signalled by 'since'

example used to make the explanation **clear**

Superhuman strength

Because of Krypton's size and mass, its gravity works out to be at least ten times as strong as Earth's.

Since lifting an object on Earth would take ten times less effort than on Krypton, Superman could lift a car as easily as we lift a wheelbarrow. It's the same reason astronauts on the Moon can take 25 metre jumps and lift huge objects with ease. Their muscles have adapted to work in the Earth's gravitational field. So the Moon's weaker gravity (one sixth the strength of Earth's) doesn't pull them back towards the surface as much.

subheading to break up the explanation into **clear steps**

causal language, signalled by 'It's the same reason'

causal language, signalled by 'so'

technical language

present tense throughout, as explaining how gravity helps Superman now

Purpose

2 Write two or three sentences to explain:

a) what the main purpose of this text is

b) what audience it is aimed at.

Give reasons for your answers. Remember to use **causal language**.

Reading for meaning

3 Explanation texts work through a series of points in a clear and logical way. Turn the explanation of Superman's strength into a flow chart, to show how the different steps are linked. You could begin like this:

> Superman comes from Krypton. But he can survive on Earth.

4 What information does the quote from *Action Comics* give (line 12)? In what way is this a 'clue' to how Superman became so strong?

5 This text includes several questions. Why has the writer used this technique?

6 Explanation texts have to use words in a precise way. These words have been used in the first paragraph of the 'Solar-powered superhero' section: 'trap', 'harvest', 'directly', 'converts'.

a) Use a dictionary to explain the meaning of each word in context.

b) Can any of these words be replaced by another without changing the meaning? Either suggest alternative words or explain why these words work best.

7 The writer could have written the text in lines 28–31 in the following way:

> Jupiter is made of gas, with only a small rocky core, so although Jupiter is 1321 times the size of Earth, it only weighs 318 times as much.

Compare this with the original text. Which is better? Why?

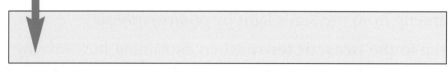

Focus on: Highlighting cause and effect

Here is an example of causal language from the website:

This is the **cause**: Jupiter is mainly gas   causal connective

Jupiter is made of gas, with only a small rocky core. *So although* Jupiter is 1321 times the size of Earth, it only weighs 318 times as much.

This is the **effect**: it is only 318 times as heavy as Earth

Causal **connectives** are used to highlight the link between cause and effect clearly for the reader. You can use many different connectives to highlight cause and effect in explanations. Here are a few:

- in order to
- when
- because
- if
- therefore
- as a result of.

8 a) Scan lines 35–47 to find four different causal connectives.

   b) Write out the whole sentence or sentences in each example. Then label the **cause**, the **effect** and the **connective** that highlights the link between the two (as in the example above).

Exploring further: Different kinds of connective

The following **connectives** can be used to highlight cause and effect links:

- **Conjunctions**, which link clauses. For example, 'The boy grew to be quick and strong, *as* his Kryptonian cells were converting the Sun's energy…'

- **Sentence connectives**, which link sentences. For example, '*So* the Moon's weaker gravity…'.

- Using nouns and verbs to make **sentence signposts**. For example, '*The fact that* Superman can survive on Earth *means that…*'

   9 Analyse the causal language in the last two sections of the website. What kind of connectives have been used?

Key Writing

 Wr12

10 a) Your task is to write an explanation for seven-year-olds of why Spider-Man can walk up walls. Use the pieces of information below to help you. Put them in a clear or logical order and use connectives to highlight each cause and effect. Produce a draft of your explanation.

- Spider-Man can stick to almost any surface.
- He can shoot silk from 'webslingers' attached to his wrists.
- Some spiders release a little bit of sticky silk on to their feet as they move.
- The silk anchors their feet in place.
- Other spiders have millions of tiny hairs on their legs.
- These slip into the nooks and crannies of a wall or window.

b) Add a short paragraph explaining why you find spiders in the bath. (Are there any nooks or crannies in a bath?)

Exploring further

 Wr1

11 Rewrite your explanation about Spider-Man so that it is suitable for an adult encyclopaedia.

- Which words, technical or otherwise, would you change?
- How would you alter the sentence structures?

③ Written in the stars?

Aims

▶ Read a text presenting arguments for and against astrology

▶ Look at how discursive texts are written and organised (S13f)

▶ Explore how to help the reader find their way around a text (S8)

▶ Identify two ways of presenting people's views (R9)

▶ Practise presenting the views of your classmates (S&L10)

The word 'myth' is sometimes used to mean a 'made-up idea'.

Your stars – science or myth?

'Your love life will take a leap forward this week…but don't make any rash decisions…' Millions of us pore over our horoscopes in newspapers and magazines. But are we just being taken in? *Out Loud* investigates…

Putting it to the test!

5 Many people have tried to prove that astrology is true. To test the astrologers' claim that Mars is the planet of male energy, risk and action, a Frenchman studied the star charts of 570 famous athletes. He was amazed to find that Mars was indeed in key

10 parts of the sky when the athletes were born.

Fun facts

♎ www.doghoroscopes.com is one of hundreds of websites that offer star charts for your pets.

♋ The earliest horoscope we have is from Babylonia (now Iraq). It dates from 409 BC.

♓ Each year over a million callers use the 'astroline' phone-ins to find out what the week has in store for them.

♓ The 12 signs of the zodiac are basically patterns in the stars. The planets move across the pattern called Aries between 21 March and 20 April each year.

Lots of tests like this have been carried out. A study of the 1991/1992 English football league, for example, suggested that players were nearly twice as likely to be born between September and November than in the summer.

But scientists fight back with tests of their own. In 2003 the scientist
15 Geoffrey Dean led his own study of 2000 people born within minutes of one another. He compared more than 100 different features, such as their anxiety levels and artistic ability. And – surprise, surprise – he found that they were not similar in any way.

Astronomer turns astrologer!

20 In 2004 a university lecturer in astronomy, Dr Percy Seymour, shocked the scientific world by publishing a book called 'The Scientific Proof of Astrology'. In it he suggests that human brain development is affected by the Earth's magnetic field, especially when the baby is in the womb. And – this is the key point – the Earth's magnetic field is interfered with by the movement of the planets.

25 Seymour's theory has met with a barrage of criticism from other scientists. "It's right up there with stuff like crop circles being made by extra-terrestrials," says Robert Massey, astronomer at the Royal Observatory.

Most scientists dismiss his arguments because the changes in the Earth's magnetic field, which are supposed to account for our behaviour, are so tiny.
30 According to one leading astronomer, you get a far stronger magnetic field from your lights and washing machine!

For or against?

We asked some of our readers what they thought about astrology.

'I believe in the Bible, not the stars. Astrology is evil.' – Elliott

'Horoscopes? You only see what you want to see in them.' – Ian

'Star signs just pigeonhole people. We're all different, aren't we?' – Kimberly

'Ha ha. You'll be believing in witches next.' – Salman

'I'm a typical Aries – independent and active. It all makes sense to me.' – Greg

'The moon affects the tides, so why can't the planets affect us too?' – Louise

'Science doesn't have all the answers!' – Chenise

'You can't judge on the basis of the star charts in magazines. A true horoscope is based on exactly where and when you were born.' – Raj

So what's the verdict? Out Loud says...

35 Hmmm … a tricky one. We'd love to *believe* in the stars, but that doesn't make it *true*. One thing we can predict, though – the 'science or myth' debate will run and run!

Key Reading

Discursive texts

This article is (mainly) a **discursive** text. Its **purpose** is to help someone understand an issue or debate by presenting the arguments fairly.

The main features of a discursive text are:

- Its form consists of an **opening statement**, a **series of points on both sides** of the issue, and a **conclusion**. For example, the first paragraph of the text introduces the issue.

- It has **sentence signposts** and **connectives** to signal which side of the issue is being written about. For example, '*Many people* have tried to prove that astrology is true'.

- It uses **formal language** in the **present tense** (expressing views that are current). For example, 'To test the astrologers' *claim* that Mars *is* the planet of male energy…'

S13f

1 The first section of the article has been annotated below, to illustrate all the features of discursive texts. Find and make a note of examples of these features for the next two sections of the article.

title in the form of a question, to show both sides of the debate

sentence signpost showing this sentence is about the 'pro-astrology' side

Your stars – science or myth?

'Your love life will take a leap forward this week…but don't make any rash decisions…' Millions of us pore over our horoscopes in newspapers and magazines. But are we just being taken in? *Out Loud* investigates…

formal language

connective showing this sentence is about the 'anti-astrology' side

present tense

Grammar for reading

A **sentence signpost** is a word or phrase at the beginning of a sentence which shows where the sentence is going, for example, 'Astrologers say…'

Purpose

2 What is the main purpose of this text? Is it:

- to entertain readers by presenting information on a hot topic
- to help someone understand both sides of the debate on astrology
- to argue that astrology isn't true?

Give reasons for your answer.

3 What is the purpose of the final paragraph? How effective is it?

Reading for meaning

4 The first paragraph of a discursive text often gives a brief introduction to the issue. This could include background information or a summary of the arguments on both sides. What kind of introduction does this article have? Support your answer with evidence from the text.

5 a) Explain why the study about English footballers was presented as evidence in favour of astrology (lines 11–13).

b) Which evidence is used to counter this argument in the next paragraph?

6 Two sentences begin with the word 'And' (lines 17 and 23).

a) What effect does this create?

b) What is the purpose of the dashes that are also used in both sentences?

7 A discursive text should give both sides of an issue roughly equal coverage. Draw up a table like the one below to analyse whether the article gives both sides a fair hearing. Complete the table for the entire article.

Paragraph/Section	Pro-astrology	Anti-astrology	Neither
Paragraph 1 (Introduction)	✓	✓	
Section: Fun facts			✓
Putting it to the test: Paragraph 2 Paragraph 3			

Using paragraphs

A discursive text has to be organised very clearly. This is because:

● the writer is giving you **more than one view** on a subject

● each view may be backed up by several **different points**.

Look at how the use of paragraphs and topic sentences makes the discussion clear for the reader.

New point: the writer now discusses 'proofs' of astrology. So a **new paragraph** is used to make this point

Topic sentence: makes it clear what the paragraph is about

Many people have tried to prove that astrology is true. To test the astrologers' claim that Mars is the planet of male energy, risk and action, a Frenchman studied the star charts of 570 famous athletes. He was amazed to find that Mars was indeed in key parts of the sky when the athletes were born.

Other sentences: back up the main point by giving examples or further details

S8

8 Present the next five paragraphs in the same way:

a) State what new point is being made.

b) How does the topic sentence make this clear to the reader?

c) What job are the other sentences doing in each paragraph?

Exploring further: Varying your sentences

9 The length of the topic sentence can make a difference to how effective it is. Look at the paragraphs in the section 'Putting it to the test!' Analyse the length of the sentences. What effect does this pattern have?

10 Rewrite the beginning of one paragraph in the next section to give it a similar effect. Which is the better version, in your opinion?

Focus on: Presenting different views

Discursive texts give the views of people from both sides of the debate. There are two main ways of doing this:

● You can **quote the views directly**:

the **reporting verb**

the **person** who said the words is named

"Horoscopes? You only see what you want to see in them" said Ian.

the **exact words** of the person are given in **inverted commas**

● You can **report the views**:

the **reporting verb** plus 'that'

the **person or people** whose views are reported

The astrologers claim that Mars is the planet of male energy, risk and action…

the **words** of the person are **reported** without using inverted commas

R9

11 Working with a partner:

    a) Find two other views that are quoted directly, and two that are reported.

    b) Present these to show the different parts of the sentence, as in the examples above.

    c) Rewrite the quoted views so that they are reported. Then rewrite the reported views so that they are quoted directly.

12 Now scan the article.

    a) How many views has the writer quoted and how many have been reported?

    b) Why are they grouped in different sections?

    c) What are the advantages of using reported speech?

Exploring further: Variety in reported speech

You can report speech in two ways:

> I believe in the Bible, not the stars. Astrology is evil.

● **Accurately**, using almost the exact words, for example, 'Elliott said that he believed in the Bible, not the stars, and that astrology was evil.'

● **In a looser way**, rewording it a bit, for example, 'Elliott condemned astrology as a great evil. He would rather believe in the Bible.'

13 a) What are the exact differences between these two versions?

   b) What are the advantages and disadvantages of each method?

14 Discuss how different reporting verbs (for example, 'claim', 'argue', 'believe') can add variety to reported speech.

Key Speaking and Listening

S&L10

15 In groups of six:

   a) Discuss what you think about astrology for five minutes.

   b) Then each decide how you could state your own view in one or two sentences.

   c) Take it in turns to state your view and listen to others' views.

   d) Finally, take it in turns to summarise the discussion.

   ● Use different phrases to report people's views.

   ● Use evidence from the discussion to support key views.

   ● Quote some of your friends' words directly, for example, 'Josh said, "Horoscopes are rubbish."'

   ● You may also want to report some people's views in a looser way, for example, 'Josh completely rubbished the whole idea of horoscopes.'

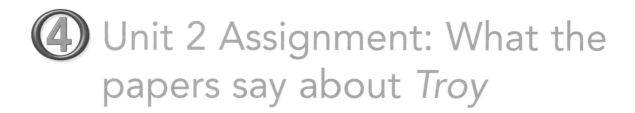

Unit 2 Assignment: What the papers say about *Troy*

Assessment Focuses

▸ **AF2**: Produce texts which are appropriate to task, reader and purpose

▸ **AF4**: Construct paragraphs and use cohesion within and between paragraphs

> **You:** are a writer for a film magazine.
>
> **Your task:** to write a summary of opinion about the film *Troy* – a 'Review of reviews'.

Stage 1

Here are some notes that you have made about the film *Troy*. Three kinds of notes are mixed up:

● extracts from the film review in *The Morning News*

● extracts from the film review in *The Evening Star*

● background information about the film.

Reorganise the notes into four paragraphs, using a chart like the one on page 49. Your fourth paragraph will be a summing up.

"Brad Pitt is a sulky, beefy hunk. He is perfect as the Greek hero Achilles." *(The Evening Star)*

Troy is based on an ancient Greek legend, as told by the poet Homer in the *Iliad*. The Greeks besiege the city of Troy to win back the stolen princess Helen.

"Achilles should be a noble figure, but Brad Pitt reduces him to a lout." *(The Morning News)*

"*Troy* is terrible. The wooden horse is great, but the wooden acting is not." *(The Morning News)*

Certificate 15, 162 minutes long.

"Give me *Gladiator* any day." *(The Morning News)*

"Movie of the year. This is a Greek version of *Gladiator*." *(The Evening Star)*

"The two and half hours raced by." *(The Evening Star)*

"There are spectacular battle sequences, political drama, and romance between Helen (Diane Kruger) and Paris (Orlando Bloom)." *(The Evening Star)*

Troy cost 200 million dollars to make.

"The romance between Paris and Helen is feeble." *(The Morning News)*

Paragraph 1: Introduction – background	
Paragraph 2: *Morning News* – views against *Troy*	**1** **2** **3**
Paragraph 3: *Evening Star* – views for *Troy*	**1** **2** **3**
Paragraph 4: Summing up	

Stage 2

Use the material in your chart to draft four paragraphs of text. Remember:

● Begin with an **introduction**.

● Give each paragraph a clear **topic sentence** that tells the reader what point you are going to make.

● Use **sentence signposts** and **connectives** to signal what point of view you are summarising.

● Present **other people's views** as **fairly** as possible.

● Use **formal** language in the **present tense**.

● Don't always **quote directly** from the newspapers. For variety, include some **summaries** in your own words.

● Add a short paragraph to **conclude** your article. You could add a comment on the different views given. You could also give your own view of the film (whether you have seen it or not!).

● Include **illustrations** with your article and add **captions** to these.

Challenge

Rewrite the review so that paragraphs 2 and 3 are organised by topic rather than by newspaper. For example, you could write one paragraph on the acting, one paragraph on the special effects, etc. How would you have to reorder your points? Which version do you think is more effective and why?

Out of this world

① Alien visitors

Aims

▶ Read an extract from a discursive text

▶ Look at how different points of view are presented

▶ Look at the way discursive texts are organised (S13f)

▶ Look at the way texts work

▶ Learn how to assess the content of a text (R8)

The following text is from a website dealing with the possibility of life on other planets.

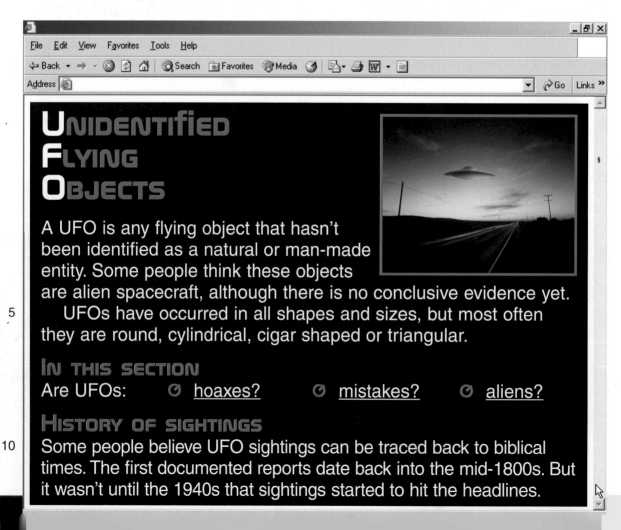

File   Edit   View   Favorites   Tools   Help

⟵ Back ⟶ ⊗ ⊡ ⌂ | 🔍 Search ☆ Favorites 🎬 Media ⟳ | ▤▾ ⊕ W ▾ ▤

Address ▐⟋   ▼ ⟳ Go | Links »

UNIDENTIFIED FLYING OBJECTS

A UFO is any flying object that hasn't been identified as a natural or man-made entity. Some people think these objects are alien spacecraft, although there is no conclusive evidence yet.

5   UFOs have occurred in all shapes and sizes, but most often they are round, cylindrical, cigar shaped or triangular.

IN THIS SECTION

Are UFOs: ⊘ <u>hoaxes?</u>   ⊘ <u>mistakes?</u>   ⊘ <u>aliens?</u>

HISTORY OF SIGHTINGS

10   Some people believe UFO sightings can be traced back to biblical times. The first documented reports date back into the mid-1800s. But it wasn't until the 1940s that sightings started to hit the headlines.

File   Edit   View   Favorites   Tools   Help

← Back ▾   → ▾ ⊗ ⊡ ⬜ | ⊘Search ⬜Favorites ⬜Media ⬜ | ⬜ ▾ ⬜ ⬜ ▾ ⬜

Address 🔳   ▼   ⟳Go   Links »

In the 1970s, Erich Von Däniken wrote a number of best-selling books saying that aliens visited the Earth long ago. Highlighting biblical references to fiery objects in the sky, he even proposed that Christ may have been an extraterrestrial. Going back even further, he suggested that ancient man had been genetically altered by aliens, explaining the 'missing link' in human evolution.

On the other hand, many scientists argue that UFOs can sometimes be explained by natural phenomena. For example, ball-lightning is often linked with UFO sightings. Some unidentified flying objects also turn out to be 'identifiable' after all. Meteorologists say that high range weather balloons are often mistaken for UFOs.

There is no doubt that unidentified objects in the sky exist. The question is – what are they? Have people witnessed alien fly-bys or something more mundane?

Are UFOs alien spacecraft?

NO	YES
There is no evidence of intelligent aliens living anywhere in our Solar System.	Many planets have been found revolving around stars outside the Solar System.
Using our current spacecraft it would take over 73,000 years to get to the nearest star system, Alpha Centauri.	Alien technology could be far in advance of our own, allowing more effective space travel.
Einstein's theory of relativity sets a limit on how fast something can travel – the speed of light. Travelling near this speed would require an enormous amount of energy.	Einstein's theory is accepted for now. But it may be wrong. More advanced theories could be discovered in the future that allow faster travel than light travel.
Officially there have been no alien spacecraft found around the world. Nearly all photographs are blurred and many have been proved to be forgeries. ↷ Find out more	There are thousands of UFO photos in the world that claim to show alien spacecraft. And many more eyewitness accounts of UFO sightings.
There are numerous other things that a UFO could be other than an alien spacecraft. ↷ Find out more	Many UFOs could be military craft or man-made objects. But witnesses include air force pilots who are trained in aerial detection.
There has been no proven scientific evidence linking the locations of sightings with unnatural phenomena. ↷ Find out more	Extra evidence has been found by witnesses in the area around UFO sightings, including debris from crashes and burn marks on the ground from landings.

15
20
25
30
35
40
45
50
55
60
65

Key Reading

> ## Discursive texts
>
> This text is a **discursive** text. Its **purpose** is to present an argument from contrasting points of view and allow you to judge between them.
>
> The main features of a discursive text are:
>
> - It has a structure that consists of an **opening statement**, a series of **points on both sides** of the issue, and a **conclusion**. For example, paragraph 1 of the web page introduces UFOs as the issue for discussion.
>
> - It uses **connectives** or **linking phrases** that signal which side of the issue you are writing about, for example, '*Some* people believe…'
>
> - It is written mainly in the **present** tense, for example, 'A UFO *is* any flying object…'
>
> - It clearly shows **evidence for each viewpoint**, for example, 'There has been no proven scientific evidence…', 'Extra evidence has been found…'

S13f

1 The extract is written mainly in the present tense but sometimes uses the past tense.

  a) Find one example in lines 13–18 where the past tense is used.

  b) What kind of information is being presented?

2 Find two pieces of evidence that UFOs can be identified from lines 19–24.

3 a) Find the linking phrases at the start of paragraphs 3 and 5 which signal that a different point of view will be described.

  b) How does the table at the end of the extract help to represent the opposing views?

4 Line 10 begins: 'Some people believe…'. How does this distance the writer from the point of view being expressed?

Purpose

5 a) Choose the main purpose of the extract from the following options:

- to convince the reader that UFOs are real
- to entertain the reader with stories of UFOs
- to put forward views from both sides of the debate and leave the reader to decide about UFOs.

b) Which other point is also true of this extract?

A **fact** is something that you can prove to be true or real. An **opinion** is what somebody thinks or believes.

6 In pairs, decide which parts of the extract give facts and which give opinions.

a) Find two facts in the extract.

b) Find two opinions.

c) In the chart, find two opinions that seem far-fetched.

d) Does the writer give his opinion anywhere in the text?

Reading for meaning

7 When were the earliest documented sightings of UFOs?

8 According to some people, how far back do UFO sightings go?

9 Find two examples of how scientists explain UFOs, one from the body of the extract and one from the table.

10 Which man-made objects have been the cause of some UFO sightings?

11 The writer asks two questions at the end of the extract.

a) What is the first question?

b) How does the second question help the reader to answer the first question?

12 What is the difference between eye-witness accounts and 'proven scientific evidence' referred to in the table? Which is more reliable as evidence?

R3

Exploring further: Using websites

13 When using a website, you can often get to the information you need more quickly than when searching for it in a book. What features of a web page allow you to do this?

14 What other pages are available on this website?

• •

Focus on: Assessing the content of discursive texts

When assessing a discursive text, you first need to identify the different views that are being presented.

15 a) Starting with the paragraphs, what are the two main points made for each view in this extract? It may help to present them in a chart like the one below:

View 1 – Points for UFOs	View 2 – Points against UFOs
First documented sightings 1880s	Explained by natural phenomena
Biblical references to fiery objects in sky	

b) Complete your chart by adding the points for and against made in the table at the end of the extract.

R8

16 Many of the main points are backed up by a piece of evidence. Find the evidence given for each point you have listed in your chart.

17 Look carefully at the points made in the chart on page 51. Analyse how well each 'No' point answers or links to each 'Yes' point. For example:

> Point 1: 'No' point effectively answers 'Yes' point by suggesting that alien life forms come from beyond our solar system.

18 The writer uses several different phrases to introduce different views. These include:
- 'Some people *think*…'
- 'Many scientists *argue*…'
- 'Erich Von Däniken *wrote*…'
- 'Meterologists *say*…'

a) Experiment with these phrases by replacing the verbs highlighted with some of the following verbs:

● suggest ● claim ● insist ● believe ● deny.

b) What difference does changing the verb make to the strength of the view being expressed?

Key Writing

19 a) In pairs, spend ten minutes discussing whether there is alien life on other planets. Try to come up with four main points for and four main points against.

You might find these points useful to start you off:
● Frequent UFO sightings in our skies.
● No response to any messages sent into space from Earth.
● Evidence of water found on Mars.
● Scientific explanations for UFO sightings.
● Potential for superior alien technology.

b) On your own, write a discursive piece entitled 'Is there life on other planets?'

Here are some words and phrases that might help you:
● 'Some people believe/think…'
● 'Others have suggested…'
● 'Whether there is life on other planets or not…'
● 'The question is…'
● 'The fact is…'

Remember to:
● start your piece by introducing your topic
● use verbs that signal different views
● create a flow between views by linking 'For' and 'Against' points
● end by asking the reader to decide what he or she thinks.

② Alien invasion

- Read the opening of a story
- Develop the skill of looking for key ideas (R8)
- Discuss the ways the text involves the reader (S&L12)
- Look at the way the text prepares the reader for the rest of the story (R15)
- Write your own introduction to a story (Wr5)

The following extract is the opening of a novel called *Only You Can Save Mankind* by Terry Pratchett.

The Hero with a Thousand Extra Lives

Johnny bit his lip, and concentrated.

Right. Come in quick, let a missile target itself – *beep beep beep beebeebeebeeb* – on the first fighter, fire the missile – *thwump* – empty the guns at the fighter – *fplat fplat fplat fplat* – hit fighter No. 2 and take out its shields
5 with the laser – *bwizzle* – while the missile – *pwwosh* – takes out fighter No. 1, dive, switch guns, rake fighter No. 3 as it turns *fplat fplat fplat* – pick up fighter No. 2 in the sights again up the upcurve, let go a missile –
10 *thwump* – and rake it with –

Fwit fwit fwit.

Fighter No. 4! It always came in last, but if you went after it first the others would have time to turn and you'd end up in the sights of three of them.

15 He'd died six times already. And it was only five o'clock.

His hands flew over the keyboard. Stars roared past as he accelerated out of the mêlée. It'd leave him short of fuel, but by the time they caught up the shields would be
20 back and he'd be ready, and two of them would already

have taken damage, and ... here they come ... missiles away, wow, lucky hit on the first one, die die die!, red fireball – *swssh* – take shield loss while concentrating fire on the next one – *swssh* – and now the last one was
25 running, but he could outrun it, hit the accelerator – ggrrRRRSSHHH – and just keep it in his sights while he poured shot after shot into – *swssh*.

Ah!

The huge bulk of their capital ship was in the corner of
30 the screen. Level 10, here we come ... careful, careful ... there were no more ships now, so all he had to do was keep out of its range and then sweep in and

We wish to talk.

His finger hovered on the Fire button. Then, without
35 really looking, he moved it over to the keyboard and pressed Pause.

Then he read the manual

Only You Can Save Mankind, it said on the cover, 'Full Sound and Graphics. The Ultimate Game.'
40 A ScreeWee, heavy cruiser, it said on page 17, could be taken out with seventy-six laser shots. Once you'd cleared the fighter escort, and found a handy spot where the ScreeWee's guns couldn't get you, it was just a matter of time.
45 *We wish to talk.*

Even with the Pause on, the message still flashed on the screen.

There was nothing in the manual about messages. Johnny riffled through the pages. It must be one of the
50 New Features the game was Packed With.

He put down the book, put his hands on the keys and cautiously typed out: Die, alien scum!

No! We do not wish to die! We wish to talk!

Key Reading

Narrative texts

This text is a **narrative**. Its **purpose** is to begin a story in an entertaining way.

The main features of a narrative text are:

● It has a structure that includes an **introduction**, a **complication**, a **crisis** (where the plot comes to a high point) and a **resolution** (when things are sorted out).
Since this is the beginning of a novel, only the introduction and complication are present. However, we can think about the possible crisis and resolution from the title of the novel – *Only You Can Save Mankind*.
Introduction: We are introduced to Johnny, who is playing a computer game.
Complication: The game aliens act in an unexpected way.
Crisis: How will Johnny respond to the aliens?
Resolution: How Johnny and the aliens solve their problems.

● It has **characters** who the story is about. We often hear their words and thoughts. For example, in this part of the story, the words of the aliens are shown in italics – '*We wish to talk*.' Johnny's thoughts are also part of the story, as he thinks himself through the game: 'Right. Come in quick, let a missile target itself…'

● There is also a **narrator** who tells the story.

● It uses **powerful words**. The narrative must be interesting to read or listen to, for example, 'Stars roared past as he accelerated out of the mêlée.'

1 The story dives straight into the action of the game. How does the writer's use of very short paragraphs add to this?

2 The story uses invented words to create the sounds of the game. Find three examples of these words and explain the actions that go with them. For example, 'swssh' represents the sound of a missile exploding in paragraph 6.

3 In the extract the words of the aliens are shown in italics. How is direct speech normally shown in a story?

4 Why do the words 'Packed With' have capital letters?

5 In what ways does this story opening make you want to read on?

• •

Purpose

The purpose of a story opening is to draw the reader in.

6 With a partner, discuss how the extract does this through:
   a) how the main character, Johnny, is introduced
   b) the action-packed start of the game
   c) the use of humour, for example, 'He'd died six times already. And it was only five o'clock.'
   d) the way the mood changes once the game is interrupted.

7 a) How clear is it at the start that Johnny is playing a game?
   b) At what point does it become clear?

• •

Reading for meaning

8 How many fighters must Johnny defeat before he gets to the capital ship?

9 What two weapons does Johnny use against the aliens?

10 Apart from hitting the aliens, what else does Johnny have to think about as he plays the game?

11 What level of the game is Johnny playing at?

12 What does Johnny think the messages from the aliens are when he finds nothing to explain them in the manual?

Use of paragraphs

13 In pairs, answer these questions about paragraphing in the story.
   a) What do the very short paragraphs seem to be about?
   b) Why do you think one word is given a paragraph to itself?
   c) What effect does the use of short paragraphs have on the pace of this story opening?
   d) Are there any disadvantages of using so many short paragraphs?

Focus on: Successful story openings

The opening of a novel is very important. It is vital that it grabs the reader's interest or he or she will not read on.

Some ingredients of a good story opening are:

- Something exciting happens at the start.
- The problem (complication) is set up quickly.
- A piece of action grabs the reader's interest.
- The main character is introduced in an interesting way.

14 Which of these techniques are used in the opening of *Only You Can Save Mankind*?

S&L12

15 Discuss the following points with a partner. Decide which of the points help to involve the reader in the extract.

a) What kind of story does the title suggest?

b) How does the chapter heading 'The Hero with a Thousand Extra Lives' help to suggest a computer game?

c) What features of a computer game are included in the story?

d) Why is the message '*We wish to talk*' so unexpected?

e) How does Johnny's reaction to the message increase the reader's interest?

Be prepared to report your ideas to the rest of the class.

R15

16 a) How many *clues* does the opening of *Only You Can Save Mankind* give about how the story will develop?

b) Below are some ways in which the story might develop. Choose the one you consider to be the best from these options. Refer to clues from the extract to support your ideas.

- Johnny will respond to the aliens' message.
- Johnny will help rescue the aliens from danger.
- Johnny will help to save the world.
- Johnny will ignore the aliens' message.
- The aliens will be hostile.

Exploring further: Punctuating clearly

Punctuation can give a clear indication of how the pauses in a passage should work.

S3

17 Read lines 21–27 of the text, paying particular attention to the punctuation.

In these lines the writer uses a series of **dashes** (–), **commas** (,) and **ellipses** (…) to separate out different parts of a very long sentence.

a) How are the sound effects marked off?

b) Apart from commas, what punctuation is used to show a pause?

c) What is unusual about the section 'die die die!'?

d) What is the effect of packing so much into a single sentence?

Key Writing

18 a) Use the table below to help you plan an exciting opening to a story.

An interesting title	
Start with an exciting piece of action	
Set up a problem (complication) quickly	
Include an event that grabs the reader's attention	
Introduce the main character(s) in an interesting way	

b) Show your plan to a partner. Ask your partner how he or she thinks the story will develop.

Wr5

c) Write your story opening in four to five paragraphs.

- Use powerful words to describe your main character.

- Include some dialogue (words from your characters) to engage the reader.

- Use punctuation so that any detailed description of events is clear.

③ Real aliens

> Read a text about aliens
> Think about audiences for texts
> Look at how information texts are put together (S13a)
> Compose your own information text

The following text is from a book about life on other planets.

Alien Life

The features of living things on Earth have arisen by evolution – a long, slow process by which living things adapt to their environment. Feathers, leaves, flowers, legs, feet and eyes, and even blood and bones, have evolved over millions of years in the particular conditions found here on Earth. So it's unlikely that on other planets there are creatures which look like donkeys or slugs. Flowers and trees are likely to be unique to Earth too.

So alien life probably wouldn't look anything like the plants and animals that we know. And it is even less likely to resemble human beings. Jack Cohen, an evolutionary biologist and author, says that he doesn't believe UFO stories about little green men – not because they are little and green, but because they are men. It is unlikely, though not impossible, that aliens would be humanoid as they so often are described in stories of close encounters.

Can we make any guesses about what alien life might look like? Living things on other planets will probably have evolved to suit their environment, as they have done on Earth. But the conditions on other planets or moons are likely to be quite different to those on Earth, so any life there would also be very different. Life on Earth depends on a mixture of nitrogen, oxygen, carbon dioxide and water vapour, but another planet's atmosphere might contain lots of methane and ammonia gases, or a mist of sulphuric acid.

A large planet has a stronger gravitational pull than a small one. Creatures living on such a planet wouldn't survive well with long, thin legs. Perhaps small creatures would evolve there.

5
10
15
20
25

Sulphuric acid can be highly corrosive. On a planet with sulphuric acid in the atmosphere, no creature like any on Earth would survive. A thick, outer covering would be a must for any living thing there.

30 Some planets have no real surface at all – they are made of gases. Jupiter and Saturn are examples of such 'gas giants' in our own Solar System. Living things on this planet would have to be buoyant, like a hot air balloon, or have wings to stop themselves from falling down to the hot, dense centre of the planet.

35 There are creatures living on Earth that might help us to predict what alien life might be like. These strange creatures are called extremophiles, which means they live in extreme conditions.

For example, there are tiny animals living inside some volcanoes. These organisms are quite different from any other life on Earth. Their staple diet consists mainly of sulphur and lots of
40 heat. These are the sort of conditions that might exist on a planet or a moon somewhere.

Strange life forms have been found living near underwater volcanoes known as black smokers on Earth. Similar volcanoes might be found on Jupiter's moon Europa. There may be life in
45 vast oceans hidden below Europa's cracked surface.

Real aliens would probably not be humanoid, such as those shown in movies like Mars Attacks!, *below.*

Key Reading

Explanation texts

This text is (mainly) an **explanation**. Its **purpose** is to help someone understand how something might work or why something could happen.

The main features of an explanation text are:

- It has a series of **clear and logical steps**. For example, 'The features of living things on Earth have arisen by evolution' highlights the first point to be explained.

- It has **causal language** that shows how one thing causes another, for example, '*So* alien life probably wouldn't look anything like…'

- It has **precise vocabulary**; technical terms may be explained in a glossary, for example, 'stronger *gravitational pull*'.

- It is written in the **present tense** when the text is explaining how or why something is now, for example, '…*says* that he *doesn't believe* UFO stories…'

- **Modal verbs** are sometimes used when discussing possibility, for example, '…another planet's atmosphere *might* contain lots of…'

- It often has **illustrations** or **diagrams** to illustrate points being explained.

S13a

1 Give the reason why it is unlikely that you would find 'donkeys or slugs' on another planet (line 6).

2 What short connective is used to show the logical conclusions in paragraphs 1 and 2?

3 Find three more scientific terms in the explanation.

4 Identify another example of the use of the present tense to explain how something is now.

Grammar for reading

Connectives are words that show how one sentence or clause is connected to another. For example, 'and', 'so', 'therefore', 'but'.

Purpose

The purpose of this explanation text is to explain some complex ideas about how life forms develop in a simple way.

5 With a partner, discuss how well the text explains these ideas. Think about its use of:

a) examples to illustrate each point

b) connectives to point to key ideas.

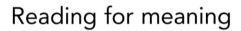

Reading for meaning

6 Why might life forms be different on different planets?

7 What kinds of alien would you expect on a planet with strong gravity?

8 What life forms might you find on a planet made up of gases?

ET – another humanoid alien.

9 Write short glossary entries for the following terms, based on the explanations given in the text:

● evolution ● extremophiles ● black smokers.

Exploring further: Scientific language

This text uses many **technical** or **scientific** terms. Many of these terms have a 'scientific' and an 'ordinary' meaning.

10 Copy out and complete the chart below by giving the scientific and ordinary meanings of each term. For the two-word terms, write down the ordinary meanings of the individual words.

Term	Ordinary meaning	Scientific meaning
Environment		
Atmosphere		
Close encounters		
Corrosive		
Staple diet		

Focus on: The structure of an explanation text

This explanation text is organised to show the reader a clear and logical progression of ideas. The flow chart below shows how the main ideas in the text are ordered.

> Life on Earth developed through evolution.

> Life on Earth developed to fit in with Earth's conditions.

> Different planets have different conditions.

> Life on other planets will be different.

> Examples of how life on other planets might fit into the environments there.

> Examples of life forms in extreme environments on Earth.

> Life on other planets will be different.

 11 In groups, discuss how you could arrange these ideas into a different order. For example, could you begin with the idea of different life forms for different planets?

12 Unlike most scientific explanations, this extract is about something that *may not* exist. The writer makes use of language that shows the **possibility** of these ideas, such as:

- might be
- probably
- perhaps
- is likely to be
- it's unlikely that
- would be.

a) Find these phrases in the text.

b) Make a note of the main idea that each word or phrase is linked to.

Key Writing

13 Write a short explanation about one of these things that doesn't actually exist:

- my ideal room
- my ideal school
- my ideal holiday.

You will need to explain:

- what the thing you are describing might look like
- what would make it special
- what its advantages would probably be.

Remember to:

- Explain your subject in clear, logical steps.
- Use causal language (for example, 'because', 'so', 'therefore').
- Use the language of possibility (modal verbs such as 'could', 'would', 'might').

④ Unit 3 Assignment: Science writing

Assessment Focus

▶ AF3 Organise and present whole texts effectively, sequencing and structuring information, ideas and events

---

You: are a science writer.

Your task: to write an explanation text about an alien of your invention for an encyclopaedia.

Your audience: young teenagers.

You need to decide:

● how you will address your audience

● how formal your language will be

● whether diagrams will be useful.

Stage 1

Choose an alien from one of these planets:

● a planet with weak gravity

● a very dark planet

● a planet with intense radiation problems

● a planet with a poor atmosphere.

Make notes about how your alien has adapted to the conditions on its planet.

Now sketch how your alien might look on its home planet.

Stage 2

Think about how to organise the ideas in
your text. Include:

- a brief introduction on why life forms
  will be different on different planets
- a description of how your alien looks
- an explanation of how your alien has
  adapted to the conditions on its planet
- a labelled illustration of your alien
- other illustrations to show your alien in
  its home environment
- a short glossary, to give a fuller
  definition of any scientific terms used
  in your explanation.

Stage 3

Remember to use the language of an explanation text. Include:

- **causal language** that shows how one thing causes another
- **precise vocabulary** and technical terms that may be explained in
  the text
- the **present tense** when describing things as they are now.

Now add words and phrases that **express the possibility** of your ideas,
such as 'might be', 'unlikely to be', 'would be', 'probably' and 'possibly'.

Challenge

Create a second alien from the same planet that has adapted
differently to its environment.

- Add a short explanation of this alien to your page.
- Use connectives to explain how and why it contrasts with the
  first alien.

Unit 4 A life of crime

① Camp Green Lake

Aims

- Read the opening from the story *Holes*
- Learn what 'literal' and 'inference' mean (R8)
- Learn how the writer keeps the reader interested (Wr7)
- Learn how to use modals to write reflectively
- Vary your sentences
- Write your own story opening (Wr5, Wr14)

This is the beginning of the story *Holes* by Louis Sachar. It is set in Texas. As you read it, try to imagine what Camp Green Lake is like.

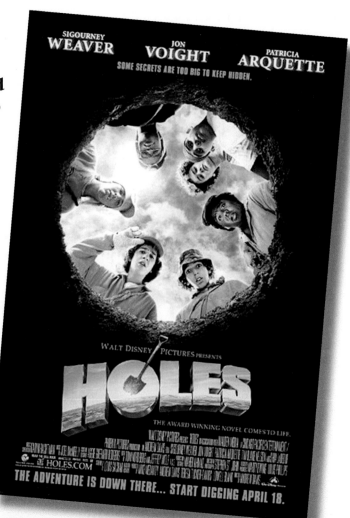

Holes

1

There is no lake at Camp Green Lake. There once was a very large lake here, the largest in Texas. That was over a hundred years ago. Now it is just a dry, flat wasteland.

There used to be a town of Green Lake as well. The town shrivelled and dried up along with the lake, and the people who lived there.

During the summer the daytime temperature hovers around ninety-five degrees in the shade – if you can find any shade. There's not much shade in a big dry lake.

The only trees are two old oaks on the eastern edge of the "lake." A hammock is stretched between the two trees, and a log cabin stands behind that.

The campers are forbidden to lie in the hammock. It belongs to the Warden. The Warden owns the shade.

Out on the lake, rattlesnakes and scorpions find shade under rocks and in the holes dug by the campers.

Here's a good rule to remember about rattlesnakes and scorpions: If you don't bother them, they won't bother you.

Usually.

Being bitten by a scorpion or even a rattlesnake is not the worst thing that can happen to you. You won't die.

Usually.

Sometimes a camper will try to be bitten by a scorpion, or even a small rattlesnake. Then he will get to spend a day or two recovering in his tent, instead of having to dig a hole out on the lake.

But you don't want to be bitten by a yellow-spotted lizard. That's the worst thing that can happen to you. You will die a slow and painful death.

Always.

If you get bitten by a yellow-spotted lizard, you might as well go into the shade of the oak trees and lie in the hammock.

There is nothing anyone can do to you anymore.

2

The reader is probably asking: Why would anyone go to Camp Green Lake?

Most campers weren't given a choice. Camp Green Lake is a camp for bad boys.

If you take a bad boy and make him dig a hole every day in the hot sun, it will turn him into a good boy.

That was what some people thought.

Stanley Yelnats was given a choice. The judge said, "You may go to jail, or you may go to Camp Green Lake."

Stanley was from a poor family. He had never been to camp before.

71

Key Reading

Narrative texts

This text is a **story opening** from a **narrative**. The **purpose** of a narrative is to entertain us.

The main features of a narrative text are:

● It has a structure that includes an **introduction**, a **complication**, a **crisis** (where the plot comes to a high point) and a **resolution** (when things are sorted out).

● It has **characters**, who the story is about. We often hear their words and thoughts.

● There is also a **narrator**, who tells the story. The story can be told in the first person (I) or the third person (he/she/they). For example, in *Holes* the narrator gives the reader a tip: 'Here's a good rule to remember about rattlesnakes and scorpions…'

● It uses **powerful words**. The narrative must be interesting to read or listen to, for example, 'The town shrivelled and dried up along with the lake.'

Story openings describe one of these:

● a character

● a place (**setting**)

● something happening (an **event**).

1 What kind of story opening is used for *Holes*?

2 a) The author uses a range of tenses in Chapter 1. Find an example of the past and present tenses.

b) What is the author referring to when he uses these tenses?

3 Is the story told in the first or third person? Support your answer with evidence from the text.

Purpose

The purpose of a story opening is to engage the reader.

Wr7

4 a) In Chapter 1 the author makes the reader feel curious.

- What are you curious about? (There may be more than one thing.)
- How does the author do this? Write a few sentences to explain your answer.

b) What important information is the reader given about Camp Green Lake in Chapter 2? What effect does withholding this information until Chapter 2 have on the reader?

Reading for meaning

When a story opens with a setting, the reader needs to feel as if he or she is there. The writer may create powerful pictures (**images**) by using nouns, adjectives and verbs. These set the mood or **tone**.

Look at how Camp Green Lake is described in the opening of *Holes*:

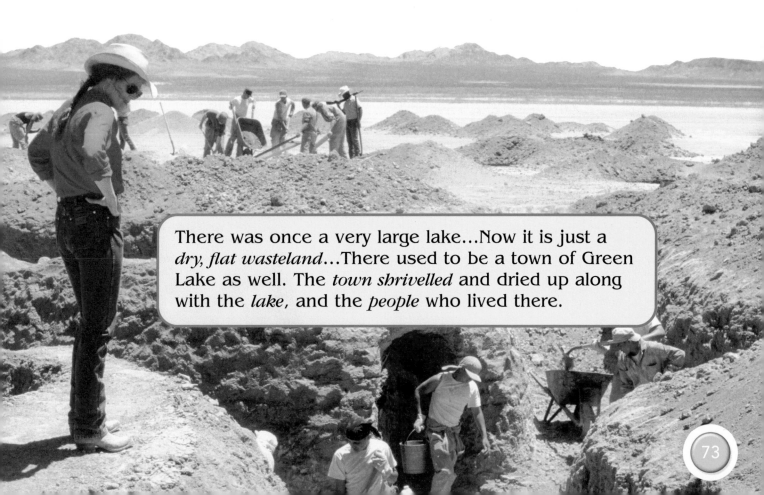

There was once a very large lake…Now it is just a *dry, flat wasteland*…There used to be a town of Green Lake as well. The *town shrivelled* and dried up along with the *lake*, and the *people* who lived there.

R12

5 a) Draw up a table with three columns, headed 'Noun', 'Adjective' and 'Verb'. In column 1, list only the nouns from the extract on page 73. (Leave enough space to write in another noun later.)

b) There are several adjectives and verbs that have similar meanings (**synonyms**) to those in the extract. However, some words suit the sentences better than others do.

W15

● Use a thesaurus to find a range of adjectives and verbs to replace those used in the extract.

● Remember, you need to find a verb similar to 'shrivelled' to suit *the town*, *the lake* and *the people*.

c) Choose the best synonyms and write them in the table.

Exploring further: Developing your sentences

6 a) Read this sentence and add 'temperature' to the 'Noun' column of your table:

> **During the summer the daytime temperature hovers around ninety-five degrees in the shade.**

b) In the same way as in question 5, find suitable verbs to replace 'hovers' and write them down.

c) Write a short descriptive paragraph, of about five sentences, for a story opening. The story is called 'Wasteland'.

● Use some of the words you have recorded in your table to create images.

● Try to find an adjective or verb to suit more than one noun.

Focus on: Knowing and inferring

When we read a text there is usually information we can be sure of. This is **literal** information. For example:

> Out on the lake, rattlesnakes and scorpions find shade under rocks...

However, we may have to pick up clues or **infer** what other information means:

> Here's a good rule to remember about rattlesnakes and scorpions: If you don't bother them, they won't bother you.
>   Usually.

R8

7 a) In the above example, something else is inferred by the word 'usually'. What do you infer from it?

b) Find the sentence, 'There is nothing anyone can do to you anymore' (line 31). What do you infer from this? There may be more than one thing. Read the previous sentence to help you.

We have seen that sometimes the author will hold back important information. Remember that the reader is not told what Camp Green Lake really is until Chapter 2. However, the reader is given clues in Chapter 1 that all is not well.

8 Write a statement about each of the following, based on what you inferred in Chapter 1 and using evidence from the extract:
- the campers
- the Warden
- the wildlife.

Exploring further: Short sentences

Look again at the sentence with only one word: 'Usually' (lines 18 and 21). It follows a long sentence. This helps to emphasise the 'danger'.

9 Add a one-word sentence underneath your 'Wasteland' description from question 6. It should infer that things are not as they should be. You may need to alter the preceding sentences to create the best effect.

Exploring further: Using the modal verb 'will'

The modal verb 'will' can be used in different ways to create different meanings. Some of the most common uses are:

- To express an **intention**, for example, 'I will go tomorrow.'
- To **consent** or agree, for example, 'I will go to the match with you.'
- To express an **inevitable** situation (something that is bound to happen), for example, 'I will miss the train.'

In the following extract from Chapter 2 of *Holes*, 'will' is used to express the inevitable:

> If you take a bad boy and make him dig a hole every day in the hot sun, it will turn him into a good boy.
> That was what some people thought.

Here we infer the statement may not be true

10 Imagine that you are a harsh warden at the camp. Write a statement using 'will' in the same way. Then add a comment that challenges it.

Key Writing

11 a) Write two paragraphs (about 200 words in total) of a story opening. The first paragraph should describe a room. Do not reveal that it is a cell until the end of the paragraph. Include small clues that it is a cell but give nothing away until the end.

- Begin by making a list of things about your cell and create images using nouns, verbs and adjectives to describe them.
- Write in the third person, past tense (and give your character a name, if you wish).

b) In the second paragraph, shift to the first person present tense. Reveal that the person in the first paragraph is you looking back. Describe your situation, thinking about where you are now. Is it better or worse? For example, 'Now, as I look back on my time in that cell, I cannot believe...'

Remember:
- At the end of the first paragraph, include sentences that suggest things are not quite what they seem.
- In the second paragraph, use modals to reflect on your situation.
- End with a one-word sentence, if you wish.

② Should music take the rap?

Aims

▶ Read an example of discursive writing (S13f)

▶ Use key words to find the main points and different points of view (R1, R7)

▶ Learn how to express complicated ideas (Wr12)

▶ Write your own point of view

▶ Use speech punctuation to quote from the text (S7)

Read the following article from the BBC Collective website.

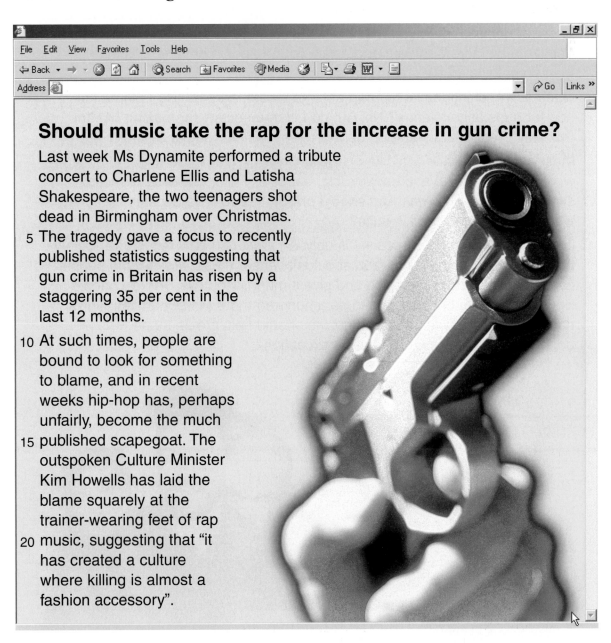

Should music take the rap for the increase in gun crime?

Last week Ms Dynamite performed a tribute concert to Charlene Ellis and Latisha Shakespeare, the two teenagers shot dead in Birmingham over Christmas.

5 The tragedy gave a focus to recently published statistics suggesting that gun crime in Britain has risen by a staggering 35 per cent in the last 12 months.

10 At such times, people are bound to look for something to blame, and in recent weeks hip-hop has, perhaps unfairly, become the much

15 published scapegoat. The outspoken Culture Minister Kim Howells has laid the blame squarely at the trainer-wearing feet of rap

20 music, suggesting that "it has created a culture where killing is almost a fashion accessory".

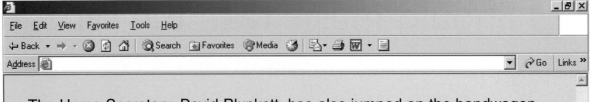

The Home Secretary, David Blunkett, has also jumped on the bandwagon,
25 stating in a recent interview, "I am concerned that we need to talk to the record producers, to the distributors, to those who are actually engaged in the music business about what is and isn't acceptable." His comments have led to an outcry in the press about the censorship of music and whether politicians should be dictating popular culture.

30 Blunkett has also been widely condemned for using music as an excuse for a much bigger problem. John Pandit of Asian Dub Foundation and Community Music, a project which offers music education in deprived areas, believes: "If David Blunkett spent as much time looking at the situations that cause crime – drugs, unemployment, bad housing and lack
35 of opportunities – then you might see a difference in the crime figures. They're a bit more pertinent about why young people get involved in crime than something they've heard on a record."

Quest Love, of influential hip-hop act The Roots, agrees: "Do I blame hip-hop for guns and violence? No. But do I blame society for making hip-hop
40 that way? Yes. Should hip-hop be more responsible with its outlook? Yes."

Most agree that while acts like So Solid Crew do glamorise guns, to censor would be impractical and unworkable, especially with the ease of music-swapping on the Internet. And should artists' freedom be decided by some white, middle-aged men in suits?

45 John Pandit: "Sometimes society is ugly. An artist can only reflect the society they are in," he says simply. "You shouldn't censor music. You get the people using music as a positive force and give it more resources. There's people like Ms Dynamite but there could be a hundred more Ms Dynamites. She's done it out of her own hard graft but we should help create those
50 opportunities. They shouldn't be the exception."

Asian Dub Foundation

Key Reading

Discursive texts

This text is a **discursive** text. The **purpose** of discursive writing is to present an argument from different points of view.

The main features of a discursive text are:

- It has a structure which consists of an opening **statement**, a series of **points** on both sides of the issue supported by **evidence**, and a **conclusion**.

- It uses **sentence signposts** to signal which side of the issue you are writing about, for example, 'Quest Love, of…The Roots, agrees…'

- It uses **formal language** in the **present tense**, for example, '…people *are bound* to look…'

S13f

1 Most discursive writing opens in the present tense. What tense is the first sentence of this article written in? Why do you think this is?

In the last paragraph, **modal verbs** are used to express complicated ideas. For example, '…to censor *would* be impractical…' Modal verbs encourage the reader to think about possibilities and to express opinions.

2 Find other examples of modal verbs, similar to 'would', that are used in the final paragraph.

Purpose

The **title** of a text can tell us what it is about. Finding **key words** in the title can help us to do this.

3 a) Which word has a double meaning in the title of the article? Explain the double meaning.

b) Write a sentence to explain what the title really means.

Reading for meaning

The **opening paragraph** of a discursive text is often used to present the **main points**. The opening paragraph of the article tells us several things:

- Ms Dynamite performed a tribute concert.
- The concert was for Charlene and Latisha.
- Charlene and Latisha were shot dead in Birmingham.
- Gun crime has risen by 35 per cent.

How can you tell what the paragraph focus is? The writer has used **sentence signposts** to show this.

> The tragedy gave a focus to…gun crime in Britain…

Gun crime has risen

Charlene and Latisha's deaths

 R1

4 a) Read the second paragraph of the article and identify the *key words* that tell you the main point.

 R7

b) Use the key words to explain to a partner what the main point of the article is.

c) Find the *sentence signpost* that links the second paragraph with the first paragraph.

Focus on: Points of view

In the article, people give their points of view about whether or not rap is the cause of the increase in gun crime. For example, there are key words that tell us what Kim Howells thinks in paragraph 2:

> … [rap] has created a culture where killing is almost a fashion accessory.

5 a) Draw up a chart like the one below. Write 'Kim Howells' in either the 'Agrees' or 'Disagrees' column.

b) Then write what he says in the third column.

Rap is the cause of an increase in gun crime.		
Agrees	**Disagrees**	**What he or she says**

6 Find other evidence in paragraph 3 to support Kim Howell's view. Identify key words to help you. Add the evidence to your chart.

7 Look through the rest of the article and identify different people's points of view. Complete your chart to show whether each person agrees or disagrees that rap is the cause of an increase in gun crime, giving evidence from the article for each point of view.

8 a) Reread paragraph 6 of the article. It discusses So Solid Crew. Find the key words that tell you about the group's attitude to guns.

b) Two points are made about whether So Solid Crew's music should be censored or not. The first point suggests that trying to censor music would be 'impractical and unworkable'. Find the key words that tell you why in the final paragraph.

9 a) What is the second point that is made about musicians' rights to play their own music? Again, find the key words that tell you, including the modal verb.

b) Do you agree with the article's last point? Write two sentences to explain your point of view. Use modal verbs.

Grammar for reading

In question 2 you looked at some verbs that help to express more complicated ideas, about what *might* happen. These are called **modal verbs**. Some examples of modal verbs are 'could', 'should', 'would' and 'might'.

Exploring further: Quoting the evidence

When you are making a point in discursive writing, you may need to support it by referring to the evidence. If you are going to quote the actual comment made, it should be enclosed in speech marks. Stylistically, you can do this in two ways:

● The actual words spoken are enclosed in double speech marks. An ellipsis (three dots) is used to show that some of the actual words have been left out. For example:

> Politicians are clearly worried and David Blunkett feels the "need to talk to the record producers…about what is and isn't acceptable."

● The written comments are enclosed in single speech marks, for example:

> Hip-hop it seems is taking the blame. As the writer comments, it has 'become the much published scapegoat.'

S7

10 Choose suitable quotes from the article and write two examples of your own using double and single speech marks.

· ·

Key Writing

Wr12

11 Write a discursive piece about whether rap is the cause of an increase in gun crime.

a) Begin with an introductory statement, saying what the main issue is.

b) Then write about:

● the different points of view made in the article, both for and against this argument

● additional comments made (for example, in paragraph 5)

● whether musicians should have the right to play whatever they like.

c) Finally, write a conclusion expressing your own point of view.

Remember to use **key words** to introduce each main point, to **quote evidence** from the article to back up each point and to use **sentence signposts** to link your paragraphs.

③ Poems and lyrics

Aims

▹ Read a poem and a series of lyrics
▹ Learn about poetic form (R14, R19)
▹ Learn about formal and informal language (S15)
▹ Write a poem or series of lyrics (Wr8)
▹ Discuss similarities and differences (S&L10)

In this poem by Allan Ahlberg, Derek Drew is always in trouble.

THE TRIAL OF DEREK DREW

The charges
Derek Drew:
For leaving his reading book at home.
For scribbling his handwriting practice.
5 For swinging on the pegs in the cloakroom.
For sabotaging the girls' skipping.
For doing disgusting things with his dinner.

Also charged
Mrs Alice Drew (née Alice Jukes):
10 For giving birth to Derek Drew.
Mr Dennis Drew:
For aiding and abetting Mrs Drew.
Mrs Muriel Drew and Mr Donald Drew:
For giving birth to Dennis Drew, etc.
15 Mrs Jane Jukes and Mr Paul Jukes:
For giving birth to Alice Jukes, etc.
Previous generations of the Drew and Jukes families:
For being born, etc., etc.

Witnesses

20 'He's *always* forgetting his book.' Mrs Pine.
'He *can* write neatly, if he wants to.' Ditto.
'I seen him on the pegs, Miss!'
'And me!' 'And me!' Friends of the accused.
'He just kept jumpin' in the rope!' Eight third-year girls
25 In Miss Hodge's class.
'It was disgusting!' Mrs Foot (dinner-lady).

For the Defence
'I was never *in* the cloakroom!' Derek Drew

Mitigating circumstances
30 This boy is ten years old.
He asks for 386 other charges to be taken into consideration.
'He's not like this at home,' his mother says.

The Verdict
Guilty.

The sentence
35 Life!
And do his handwriting again.

Below are the lyrics of a song by Elvis Costello telling the true story of nineteen-year-old Derek Bentley. In 1953 he was found guilty of the murder of a policeman who was attempting to arrest him and his accomplice Chris Craig.

Let Him Dangle

Bentley said to Craig "Let him have it Chris"
They still don't know today just what he meant
by this
Craig fired the pistol, but was too young to swing
5 So the police took Bentley and the very next thing
Let him dangle
Let him dangle

Bentley had surrendered, he was under arrest,
when he gave Chris Craig that fatal request
10 Craig shot Sidney Miles, he took Bentley's word
The prosecution claimed as they charged them
with murder
Let him dangle
Let him dangle

15 They say Derek Bentley was easily led
Well what's that to the woman that Sidney
Miles wed?
Though guilty was the verdict, and Craig had
shot him dead
20 The gallows were for Bentley and still she
never said
Let him dangle
Let him dangle

Well it's hard to imagine it's the times that
25 have changed
When there's a murder in the kitchen that is
brutal and strange
If killing anybody is a terrible crime
Why does this bloodthirsty chorus come round
30 from time to time?
Let him dangle

Not many people thought that Bentley would
hang
But the word never came, the phone never rang
35 Outside Wandsworth Prison there was horror
and hate
As the hangman shook Bentley's hand to
calculate his weight
Let him dangle

40 From a welfare state to society murder
"Bring back the noose" is always heard
Whenever those swine are under attack
But it won't make you even
It won't bring him back

45 Let him dangle
Let him dangle (String him up)

Key Reading

Poetry/Lyrics

The first text is a **poem**; the second is a set of **song lyrics**. Their **purpose** is to explore feelings and ideas.

They are both made up of **images**, **rhythm** and **form**.

● The **images** are the pictures made by the words.

● The **rhythm** is like the beat in music.

● The **form** is the framework or pattern. Poems and lyrics are written in **lines** not sentences.

Other important features are:

● Some poems **rhyme**, for example, doom/gloom/tomb.

● Some poems are **free verse**. They have lines of different lengths with different rhythms. (Some free verse contains rhyme.)

● Lyrics usually rhyme and have a strong rhythm.

● Lyrics often have repeating lines (a **refrain**).

1 Poets use all kinds of situations or contexts to give their work form. What context has Allan Ahlberg used in *The Trial of Derek Drew*? How do you know?

2 *The Trial of Derek Drew* is a free verse poem. How does *Let Him Dangle* differ in this respect?

Purpose

The Trial of Derek Drew explores all the things that Derek has done wrong at school. However, it is a funny or **comic** poem. Why do you think this is?

3 a) Look at the first verse, 'The charges', which tells you what Derek has done wrong. Would you call what Derek has done 'crimes'? Why?

b) Think about what Derek has done and why the poem is funny. Write two sentences to explain why the poem is a comic poem using both of these verbs:

● contrast ● exaggerate.

4 a) Why do you think Elvis Costello wrote *Let Him Dangle*?

   b) In what important way is the subject of the song different from the subject of *The Trial of Derek Drew*?

• •

Reading for meaning

Formal and informal language

The Trial of Derek Drew uses **official language**, to make it seem as if Derek is in a court of law. It is the kind of language used in legal documents.

W16 **5 a)** What does each of the subheadings mean? Use the context of the verses they head to help you.

   b) Shorthand is also used. Find two examples in verses 2 and 3. What do the shorthand words mean and who or what do they refer to?

Using this kind of official language gives us a clear picture of Derek on trial. This image adds to the humour of the poem. However, there is also **informal language** in the poem when people use their own words.

S15 **6** Find an example of informal language in the poem. How can you tell that the language is informal?

Exploring further: Brackets and colons

Brackets ( ) and colons : are also used in the poem.

● **Brackets** separate out extra information within a sentence.

● The **colon** can be used to introduce a list or to give an example within a sentence.

   7 a) Find two examples of the use of brackets in *The Trial of Derek Drew*. How do they add to the formal tone?

   b) Identify where colons are used. What is their purpose?

Exploring further: Ballads

Let Him Dangle is a **ballad** (a narrative in verse). Ballads can be songs or poems. Traditional ballads have four lines to a verse.

R19

8 Look again at the verses in *Let Him Dangle*. In what way are they different from a traditional ballad?

As with many ballads, *Let Him Dangle* is also a **commentary** – writing in which the author expresses a point of view. You need to be clear about the narrative to understand the point of view.

9 Make brief notes on the following:

  a) Which verses deal with the narrative?

  b) What are the main events and the end for Derek Bentley?

10 a) Where does the commentary begin?

  b) What is the writer's point of view? To answer this question, think about:

  ● what happened to Derek Bentley and his punishment

  ● how the writer feels about this.

Focus on: Creating form

Repetition (repeating lines or words) is used in *The Trial of Derek Drew*.

R14

11 a) Which word is constantly repeated in verses 1 and 2?

  b) What impression does this give of the court? Write down your answer.

Although the poem and the lyrics are very different in style and form, both use repetition. Lyrics often have a **refrain** or chorus. This is, in effect, repeating lines.

12 a) What is the refrain in *Let Him Dangle*? How do these repeating lines emphasise the meaning of the song?

  b) Why do you think a refrain fits well with music?

Exploring further

Wr8

13 Complete one of the following tasks:

- Write a poem using the same form as *The Trial of Derek Drew*. You could use similar subheadings above each verse. Use a dictionary and thesaurus to help you.

- Write a rap on the same theme as *Let Him Dangle*. Try out different rhymes (and if you can, perform them) before you settle on what to include.

Key Speaking and Listening

S&L10

14 In groups, compare *The Trial of Derek Drew* and *Let Him Dangle*.

a) Choose a member to draw up a 'Similarities and Differences' chart. The group should agree which points to record as the discussion unfolds.

b) Agree on the features you will compare, and make a list. For example:

- form
- theme
- use of images
- regular/irregular rhythm
- rhyming/non-rhyming.

Discuss these in order, giving everyone a chance to speak.

c) Draw on useful connectives to help you think and talk, such as:

- 'Although…'
- 'Except…'
- 'By comparison…'
- 'Apart from…'
- 'On the one hand…'
- 'On the other hand…'

d) Finally, select what you think are the most important differences and choose someone to report back to the class.

④ Unit 4 Assignment: The storyteller

Assessment Focuses

▶ AF4 Construct paragraphs and use cohesion within and between paragraphs

▶ AF7 Select appropriate and effective vocabulary

> **You**: are a storyteller.
>
> **Your task**: to write a story for other students to read.

Stage 1

Open your story with a setting.

Where?	A loft in a deserted old house.
What is it like?	It has a large, heavy door. It has a small window (skylight) in the roof.
What else?	Add to this list of ideas.

Then introduce your main character.

Who?	Your character is a criminal. Draw up a list of possible character traits. Include strengths and weaknesses. Does he or she have any redeeming traits, despite being a criminal? Give your character a name but let other features emerge as you write. For example:

> He had to place the stool on top of the chair to reach the skylight.

This action tells us that the character is not very tall

Now think of another character *that you will introduce later*. Have a rough idea of what he or she is like. For example, will he or she be friendly or a threat to your main character? Is he or she clever? Could he or she be misled by your character?

Stage 2

What happens?	Think of a problem for your main character. Why is he or she in the loft? Perhaps your character is looking for something? Does he or she find something else instead? Does this pose a dilemma?

Introduce your second character at this point.
- What does he or she do?
- What does your main character do in response?

Stage 3

What is the ending?	What happens to your character? Does he or she solve the problem? If yes, then how? What happens to the second character? Does the story have a happy or a sad ending?

Use your plan as a guide to write your story. You can change it as you write if you think of better ideas.
- Write descriptive sentences.
- Vary the length of your sentences to add variety and pace to your writing.
- Ask questions as well as making statements. For example, instead of writing: 'He didn't know what to do next', you could write: 'What could he do now?'.

Challenge

Include a magic or horror element in your story. Decide:
- where you introduce it
- what causes the change
- who or what it affects (for example, your main character)
- how you will describe what is happening
- how you will signal it on the page. For example, you could write in another coloured pen or use italics on the keyboard to distinguish fantasy from reality.

Remember not to make the fantasy too far-fetched. The reader needs to remain engaged with your story.

① Two Weeks with the Queen

Aims

▶ Read the beginning of a play (R18)

▶ Learn about how plays are set out

▶ Develop ideas about characters and how to perform (S&L15)

▶ Write a short section from a play

The following extract is from the opening to a play by Mary Morris, based on the novel *Two Weeks with the Queen* by Morris Gleitzman.

The music of God Save the Queen is heard, followed by the plummy voice of her Majesty delivering her Christmas message.
At the Mudfords' place Mum and Dad, barefoot and dressed in shorts, singlet and paper hats, are fanning themselves with a bit torn off a beer carton. They are watching the Queen's Christmas message on TV. Colin, also in shorts and very scuffed brown elastic-sided boots,
5 *sits some way from them glaring at an open shoe box containing a pair of sensible black school shoes. His kid brother Luke runs in and out strafing everybody and everything with his new MiG fighter plane. Colin picks up a shoe and looks at it with distaste.*

QUEEN   And a very merry Christmas to you all.

10 COLIN   Merry flamin' Christmas. [*Luke strafes him*] Gerroff!

LUKE   Wanna go?

COLIN   Get lost.

Luke does a circle of the room shooting down the enemy and swoops on Colin again.
Colin throws a shoe at him.

15 LUKE   He hit me! Dad, he hit me!

DAD   Don't hit your brother, Colin.

COLIN   I didn't…

MUM   You heard your father.

COLIN   It was him, he started…

20 DAD   That's enough! We're trying to listen to the Queen here.

COLIN	Nobody ever listens to me.
LUKE	That's cos you're not the Queen.
DAD	Just keep it down to a roar, eh?

Dad snuggles Mum closer to him and they settle back with the Queen who rabbits on about equality and justice for all.

COLIN	[quietly, in Luke's direction] Lucky for you I'm not the Queen. If I was I'd have you locked in the tower and torture you and put you on the rack till your bones creak and then I'd have your fingernails pulled out one by one and then I'd pour boiling oil on you and hang you from the battlements and then I'd…
LUKE	Mum, I don't feel well.
COLIN	Then I'd have you cut open right down the middle and your guts would hang out and all the blow flies would come and the crows would peck out your eyes…
LUKE	[louder] Mum, I feel sick.
MUM	Serves you right for having four serves of chrissie pud.
COLIN	Four?! I only got three!
LUKE	I do, but. [He goes back to playing with his MiG.]
COLIN	Prob'ly a strain of heat resistant bacteria in the chrissie pud. If I'd got a microscope for Christmas instead of a pair of school shoes I could have run some tests and spotted it. We'll prob'ly all come down with it now.
DAD	Colin, go and shut the back door mate – keep some of the heat out.
COLIN	Why can't he go?
DAD	Cos I asked you to.
COLIN	Yeh, well he'd be quicker, he's got turbo thrusters, I've only got lace-ups.

Mum and Dad exchange a guilty glance.

MUM	Luke, go and shut the door. [Luke goes, Dad turns the Queen off.] Love, about the microscope…
DAD	Next time, eh?
MUM	We just couldn't stretch to it.
COLIN	I know, the recession.
MUM	Besides, you needed shoes.
COLIN	[looking at his appalling boots] No I didn't.
DAD	[picking up a shoe] They're pretty snazzy shoes. Bloke could end up Prime Minister in shoes like those.
MUM	They are the ones you liked in the shop – aren't they?
COLIN	Yes, they're, um, they're good.
MUM	Colin love, is there something else bothering you?
COLIN	[shrugging] Nuh.
DAD	You can talk to us mate, you know that.

```
        COLIN   Well…
        MUM     Yes love?
65      COLIN   It's just that… well…
        DAD     Yes?
        COLIN   Nobody ever…
        LUKE    [entering the room] Mum. Mum!
        As they turn towards Luke, he collapses on the floor. Mum and Dad rush towards him.
70      COLIN   Pays any attention to me.
        The sound of an ambulance is heard.
```

Key Reading

Play scripts

This text is a **play script**. Its **purpose** is to entertain the audience.

The main features of a play script are:

- It presents a range of **characters** – their names or roles appear on the left-hand side of the page. What they say *does not* have speech marks. For example:
  DAD   Don't hit your brother, Colin.

- Characters' **actions** or how they speak are written in the **present tense**. In this script they are presented separately from the speech, as **stage directions**. For example:
  Mum and Dad exchange a guilty glance.

- **Stage directions** are also used to set the scene. For example:
  The music of God Save the Queen *is heard…*

1 In pairs, discuss the scene.

  a) Who are the characters?

  b) What is happening in the scene?

2 Who do you think is the main character?

3 a) Find an example of a stage direction, telling a character how to behave, or what to do. Remember, this will not be speech.

  b) Find an example of a stage direction that sets the scene.

Purpose

One of the ways the writer tries to entertain us at the start of a play is by setting up a problem that the characters need to overcome. We are entertained because we want to know *how* the problem will be solved.

4 What do you think is the real problem Colin is trying to explain to his parents towards the end of the scene?

The writer interests us in other ways. For example, she gets **straight to the point of the story**. She does not waste time introducing the problem. Even before anybody speaks, we know that Colin is not happy.

5 Find a sentence in the opening stage directions that tells us Colin is unhappy.

The writer also tries to entertain us by using humour – by making us laugh.

6 a) Find two speeches by Dad that are meant to make us laugh.

b) How else does the writer use humour in this scene?

Reading for meaning

7 We learn quite a lot about the sort of life the Mudford family leads in this opening scene.

a) Find two things that tell us they do not have a lot of money.

b) Find one stage direction that shows Mum and Dad have a close relationship.

c) The scene is set in Australia. Find one speech and one stage direction that remind us the family is in Australia. (Remember that in Australia Christmas is in the summer.)

Exploring further: The writer's use of language

The writer uses a very different style for some of Colin's speeches, compared with the speeches by the other characters. These are when he is teasing Luke and telling him all the horrible things he would do to him.

8 What are the main points you notice about these speeches to Luke?

Focus on: Developing drama techniques

The actors who perform *Two Weeks with the Queen* need to know what their characters are like. One way of doing this is by looking at what the character *says*.

For example, COLIN.

What COLIN says	What this tells us about COLIN
(about the state of the house) *Merry flamin' Christmas.*	a) He's not really enjoying himself. b)
(about Luke shutting the door) *Why can't he go?*	a) b)
(about his new shoes) *Yes, they're, um, good.*	a) b)

R18

9 Copy the grid and write two things in the second column that you think Colin's speeches tell us about him, as in the example above.

Exploring further: More character pointers

We can also find out about a character by the way *others* respond to him or her.

10 How do Mum and Dad respond when Colin compares his Christmas present with Luke's (lines 46–61)? What does this tell us about how they feel about Colin?

11 Colin's lines can be said in very different ways to create different meanings. Try saying this line of Colin's in three different ways: 'I know, the recession.'

a) First, say it as if you really understand the problem your parents have.

b) Next, put stress on the word 'know' as if you are annoyed because you have heard all this before.

c) Finally, say it sarcastically, with the stress on 'recession', as if you think this is just an excuse for buying boring shoes instead of a microscope.

Decide which of these works best.

12 Read the first stage directions carefully, then look at lines 9–23. You are going to prepare this short section in groups of four.

S&L16

a) Decide between you who will play each part.

b) Think about what you have learnt about each character in this unit. This should help you decide how they will say their lines and what they will do. For example:
– Colin could be rather naughty, and rude to his little brother.
– Dad could be patient and understanding.

c) Now practise a short performance of these lines. In your performance, make sure it is quite clear what each character is like.

Key Writing

13 The extract from Scene 2 ends with the sound of an ambulance. What do you think happens next?
● Is Luke really ill?
● Does Colin carry on trying to explain what is bothering him? Or does he keep teasing Luke?
● What happens when the ambulance arrives?
● What new character might you need?

a) Write eight to ten more speeches to end the scene.

b) Include speech from Colin and Mum or Dad.

Remember:
● to place character names on the left
● not to use speech marks
● to include stage directions for what characters do.

A scene from the novel, Two Weeks with the Queen

Exploring further

14 Write the start of the next scene, where Luke has been taken to hospital. Decide where in the hospital the scene takes place, who the characters will be, what is happening to Luke and how Colin will behave.

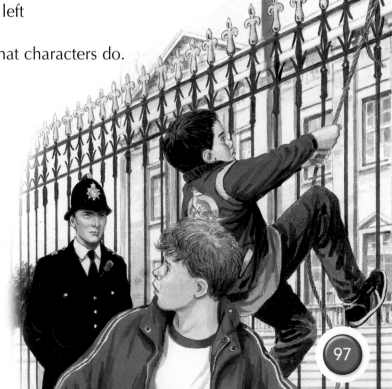

How to create a stage design

- Read a set of instructions about designing a set for a play
- Explore different ways to stage a well-known story
- Learn how to work together as a group to solve problems logically (S&L13)
- Present ideas for a set design

Creating a stage design

All plays have some sort of a stage design. Even if the design is to leave the stage blank, with no props or set, that is still a design. This is because someone has decided that is what the stage will look like. Usually this person is the Stage or Set Designer.

5   However, the Set Designer does not work alone. He or she has probably talked with the Director (the person responsible for the acting) and the Producer (the person responsible for everything else!) about the design.

10 So, how do you go about designing a set?

1. **Talk to the Director** to find out how he or she sees the play. For example, imagine the play is a fairy-tale, like *Little Red Riding Hood*. Does the Director want a *modern* design, or a *traditional* one? Sometimes directors want modern designs so
15 that audiences can 'relate' to the play. So, if they want a modern design, perhaps tall skyscrapers would be better than tall trees.

2. **Start brainstorming ideas.** It's vital to come up with a list of possible ideas to use. After all, you don't want to suggest just one idea and then find the Director doesn't like it.
20

For example:

Very traditional. Twisted old trees and a pretty cottage.

Set in a big city. Tall sky-scrapers for the forest. The wolf could even be a bearded businessman!

How about a junkyard? LRRH's granny runs it?

A hot, dry desert. Tents. Pyramids. The woodcutter is a handsome sheikh.

Little Red Riding Hood

Red curtains across the back of the stage, with one or two thin trees. The wolf peeps through holes in the curtains.

The set looks like a maze. High green hedges. LRRH is like a little princess, lost in her own garden.

Futuristic. Science-fiction. Everything white and plastic. Granny's cottage is a white box with a little window.

No set really. Just a bed in the centre of the stage. The bed is used as the cottage, the woods…whatever we want it to be.

3. Once you and the Director have decided on an idea, **sketch out how the stage will look** when the play starts. Of course, you may have different sets for each part of the play, but for now, stick to the opening. Do the sketch simply – there's no point in wasting time on making it too artistic.

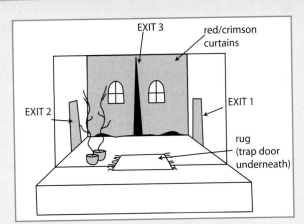

4. Once the basic design has been agreed, **write an explanation of the set** for the opening scene. You need to do this to make it clear how you see the design. This can go with the sketch, if needed.

For example:

Opening scene: Set 1
- The stage consists of two, dark blood-red curtains hanging down from the back of the stage (<u>upstage</u>) to suggest blood and Little Red Riding Hood's colour.
- <u>Downstage right</u> are two thin black trees with no leaves, to suggest a withering, deadly place.
- <u>Downstage centre</u> is a dusty rug, to cover a trap door through which the wolf enters.
- The exits <u>stage right and left</u> consist of two wooden doors, which open outwards for practical reasons.

5. Next, think about, or **start planning**, any **scene changes** or new sets the play will need.

25

30

35

40

45

Key Reading

Instruction texts

This text is an **instruction** text. Its **purpose** is to tell someone clearly how to do something. At times, this text also **explains** things to the reader.

The main features of an instruction text are:

- It has a **clear design** with a **step-by-step** approach often supported by **pictures** or **diagrams**. For example, the diagram of the stage shows how to do a basic sketch.

- It has a **plain and simple** style often using **connectives** of **time** or **sequence**, for example, '*Once* you and the Director have decided on an idea, sketch out how the stage will look *when* the play starts.'

- It uses **imperative** verbs. These are verbs that **tell** (or **command**) you to do something, for example, '*Talk* to the Director.'

- It uses **technical language** when required, for example, 'Even if the design is to leave the stage blank, with no *props* or *set*…'

S13d

1 What is this text giving instructions about and who is it aimed at?

2 What visual aids are used in this text?

3 a) Points 4 and 5 both begin with time connectives. What are they?

   b) Only a few time connectives are used in this instruction text. Can you think of any other processes or subjects in which time connectives for instructions would be used more?

4 How many other imperative verbs (command words) can you find? Make a list.

5 The point is made that this is partly an explanation text. Where in the text is the writer *explaining* rather than *instructing*?

Purpose

The purpose of this text is to make the instructions clear and easy to follow. Numbering the sections helps to do this.

6 Why would it be confusing *without* the numbering?

7 What is the main purpose of the first part of the text (before the numbered section)? What information do we find out from it?

Reading for meaning

8 As you have seen, Set Designers have a range of options when preparing a 'look' for a play. Discuss why you think someone directing or producing a play about a traditional story might decide to set it in modern times?

9 In section 2, the Set Designer comes up with several different ways of staging *Little Red Riding Hood*. He or she also mentions how some of the characters might be played. Copy and complete the chart below, finding the exact reference from the text that tells you how each character might be played.

Character	How played	Reference from text
Little Red Riding Hood	Little princess	'LRRH is like a little princess, lost in her own garden.'
Granny		
Wolf		
Woodcutter		

10 Make a list of things which need to be provided for the play, for example, 'blood red curtains'. Look for the other nouns from section 4 to add to the props list.

Exploring further: Theatrical terms

11 The text ends with an explanation of the diagram of the set. The writer uses a number of technical terms used in drama and staging (these have been underlined).

   a) Find out what these terms mean.

   b) What is potentially confusing about them?

12 Here is a short description of a set design. Use it to draw a diagram of the stage.

> Upstage left there is a long sofa, with a small, round table to one side. There are flowers in a vase on it. Behind the sofa is a small picture window. Downstage right, there is a rocking chair facing towards the centre of the stage. Upstage from the chair is a desk with a small laptop on it. Upstage right is an old, battered trunk, lid open.

Focus on: Working together

Putting on any play or show at school depends on team work. This means using some special speaking and listening skills.

13 Working in small groups, imagine you have to create a set design for the beginning of *Two Weeks with the Queen* (see page 92). Once you have created it, you have to present your ideas to the class.

If you are going to produce a clear, logical plan for your set design, you must work together. Here are three important things to bear in mind when you are working as a group:

● Be clear about **what** you have to do

● Think about the **order** in which to do things

● Think about **who** will do what.

a) Below is one group's solution to planning their set design. However, it is jumbled up. In your group, put it into a logical order.

> A Agree who will keep notes of the discussion and who will report back to the Director.
>
> B Meet as a group and share ideas one by one (everyone listen!).
>
> C Decide on the design that suits the play best.
>
> D Firstly, on your own, read the play and come up with some ideas (make sure you have good reasons for suggesting them).
>
> E Then share ideas on how that design can be developed (for example: colours, props).

b) Does the new order make it clear who does what?

c) Use this plan as the basis for your own group planning. Add extra steps if you wish and be ready to present your ideas.

Key Speaking and Listening

14 Use your plan to write up a design for the *Two Weeks with the Queen* set.

a) Make **notes** for your own design first. (Look at Unit 9, which gives advice on note-making.) Include **diagrams** or **sketches** to bring your set to life. However, *don't* waste time on writing out a long description of what you want.

b) When you have finished, present your design to your group. Explain your ideas for the set.

c) Decide which would be the best design to use.

Use this short checklist to make sure you support each other when presenting and evaluating your designs:

Check	Yes	No
Did you get the chance to present your idea?		
Did you explain your ideas clearly?		
Did you listen to other people's ideas (without interrupting)?		
Did you all agree on a final design?		
Did you all contribute ideas to develop the final design?		

Exploring further

S13c

15 Now write up your group's agreed design. This will be an **explanation** text.

Remember to:

● include a **sketched design** if you wish, like the one on page 99
● use **causal connectives**, such as 'in order to', 'so as to', 'for'
● stick to the **present tense**, for example, 'The set *consists* of…'
● use **appropriate technical terms** where you can, such as 'downstage'.

③ Reviewing Nemo

Aims

❱ Read a film review

❱ Learn about the key features of reviews

❱ Speak about a film or programme you have seen (S&L19)

❱ Write a section from a review (S17)

These two film reviews come from the *Unreel* and *Tiscali* websites. As you read them, think about how they are alike and how they differ.

Review 1

Starring: Albert Brooks, Ellen DeGeneres, Alexander Gould, Willem Dafoe, Geoffrey Rush

The latest offering from the makers of 'Monsters Inc' and 'Toy Story' has broken box office records in the States for an animated feature
5 film, and it is not difficult to see why, with its fantastic story, brilliant comic moments and ground-breaking visuals.

Nemo (Alexander Gould) is a young clownfish, born with lopsided fins, and the only son of Marlin (Brooks), who has recently lost his wife and unborn children in a barracuda attack. The pair live in the
10 Great Barrier Reef, a safe existence compared to the dangers of the 'drop-off' into deep water.

Nemo's curiosity gets the better of him though, and on his first day at school he goes off into the deep, ignoring his father's warning, and ends up being captured by a scuba diver. . . eventually becoming an
15 attraction in a Sydney dentist's saltwater fish tank.

Marlin, of course, is desperate to find his son, and so enlists the help of Dory (DeGeneres), a blue tang with a desperate short-term

105

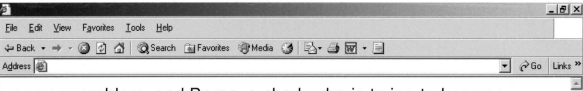

memory problem, and Bruce, a shark who is trying to become vegetarian.

20 Their mission soon becomes the stuff of legend, with everyone in the seas, and plenty more above them, seemingly aware of Marlin's strife, as he trawls the oceans for his son.

Nemo too has a mission: to escape from the aquarium. He also has some new found friends to help him, led by Moorish Idol fish, Gill
25 (Dafoe). They decide the time is right to take action when Nemo is chosen to be the new pet of Darla, a ghastly eight-year old, and enlist the help of Nigel the Pelican (Rush).

Pixar Studios have created another stunning film in 'Finding Nemo', proving that where they could conquer the difficulty of fur in
30 'Monsters Inc.' they can do the same with water. They are currently producing the finest computer-animated films around, and the key to their success is plain to see. 'Finding Nemo' is an action-filled adventure, with some great comic moments, supplied in the main by Dory and Bruce, but supported by other great characters such as
35 Crush – the 150-year-old turtle with the mind and vocabulary of a teenage surfer. It is also a touching film, with some heartwarming father/son moments. And having managed once again to bring all these elements together, the end result is quite fantastic.

File Edit View Favorites Tools Help

Back | Search Favorites Media |

Address

Finding Nemo

With *Toy Story*, Pixar's first venture into fully computer generated feature films, it was impossible not to marvel at its technical wizardry. But after fifteen minutes, when one's jaw had returned from its encounter with the floor, it was the film's wonderful characters and enjoyable plot that
5 sustained the magic. Now, eight years later, their impeccable resumé of hits, including *Monsters, Inc.* and *A Bug's Life*, have generated a high level of expectation. So it's almost inevitable that their latest collaboration with Disney is unable to satisfy such lofty anticipation.

Visually, the aquatic adventure is every bit as stunning as its
10 predecessors. The vibrant undersea world and its colourful array of wildlife is impossibly dazzling. More drab are the unmemorable characters and the lumbering plot. *Finding Nemo* is certainly not without its entertaining blend of childlike sweetness and adult wit, but in less measure than we've become used to.

15 For such a bright film its opening is decidedly dark. When the idyllic life of clownfish Marlin (Albert Brooks) is abruptly shattered, he's left to bring up his only son Nemo (Alexander Gould) on his own. Brooks can generally be relied upon to provide some angst-ridden humour, but without his hangdog face to emphasise it, he struggles to make Marlin
20 anything more than a whiny, over protective father. When the young Nemo tries to assert his independence, he is snatched from his coral reef home and whisked off to the waiting room aquarium of a Sydney dentist. It is Marlin's subsequent quest to be reunited with his son that provides the film with its title and plot.

25 In his search he is joined by the well meaning but somewhat ditzy Dory (Ellen DeGeneres) who suffers from short-term memory loss. Here, as is often the case with animated kids' movies, the central characters' job is to keep the story moving while the peripheral figures provide the humour. Dame Edna (aka Barry Humphries) is the voice of the self-
30 improving shark Bruce, who is trying to wean himself off eating his finned sea mates by way of a twelve-step program and the motto "fish are friends, not food". Geoffrey Rush clearly enjoyed his stint as the excitable pelican Nigel, and Andrew Stanton adopted the ultimate surfer dude droll for the sea turtle Crush.

35 *Finding Nemo* doesn't resist the temptation to add some fundamental moralizing about the value of family and friends, but stops just short of becoming too soppy. During the pursuit of Nemo, there are few surprises and few big laughs. What there are are some tender moments, some broad smiles and a realization that sadly even Pixar aren't invincible.

Key Reading

Reviews

Both of these texts are **film reviews**. Their **purpose** is to inform readers about the film, in an entertaining way.

Some of the features of review texts are:

- They provide **key information** about the story and characters, for example: 'Nemo…is a young clownfish.'

- They give the reader an idea of the **reviewer's opinion** of the film. This is done in a variety of ways, such as:
  - Comparison and contrast (with previous or other films)
  - Choice of language (for example, in the reviewer's descriptions of plot or characters)
  - Reference to actors or actresses and their performances.

- They use a **friendly, informal tone** – as if speaking to a fellow movie-fan, for example, '…as is often the case with animated *kids' movies*…'

- They use a wide range of sentences to pack in detail, including **noun phrases**, for example, 'Geoffrey Rush clearly enjoyed his stint as the *excitable pelican Nigel*.'

1 Clearly, both reviews are about the same film, but what obvious similarities and differences can you see between them on a first reading?

2 Now look at the key features of reviews in the box above. Can you find a specific example of each feature in the two reviews?

3 Does either review reveal – or imply – how the film ends?

Grammar for reading

If you **imply** something, you do not say it directly or give the full information. For example, a review might say, 'The film moves towards its inevitable, tragic conclusion.' This implies that the ending is sad, but it doesn't tell the reader exactly what happens.

Purpose

Both reviews **entertain** the reader because when you read them, it is like seeing snapshots of the story – a kind of mini-trailer for the film.

4 Find one example of a 'snapshot' from the film in Review 2.

We are also **informed** – not just about the story but about what the writer thinks of Pixar Studios, who made the film. For example, in Review 1:

> Pixar Studios have created another stunning film in 'Finding Nemo', proving that where they could conquer the difficulty of fur in 'Monsters Inc.' they can do the same with water. They are currently producing the finest computer-animated films around, and the key to their success is plain to see.

Shows they have the skills to do things other film studios might find difficult

5 What other words or phrases in the extract above suggest that Pixar Studios are doing a good job?

Reading for meaning

The structure of Review 1 means that the final paragraph is used to:

- sum up the overall qualities of the film
- praise Pixar Studios, the makers of the film
- give one last example of a character who hasn't been mentioned (Crush, the 150-year-old turtle).

6 Now look at Review 2. Does its final paragraph address the same elements? If it is different, describe how.

Exploring further: Using commas

In describing the events in the story, the reviewer has to pack quite a lot into each sentence. Consider this example:

> Marlin, of course, is desperate to find his son, and so enlists the help of Dory (DeGeneres), a blue tang with a desperate short-term memory problem, and Bruce, a shark who is trying to become vegetarian.

7 Look at the use of commas in the sentence above. What job are they doing? Note how the conjunction 'with' also helps to provide extra information.

8 Now look at the first sentence of Review 2:

> With *Toy Story*, Pixar's first venture into fully computer generated feature films, it was impossible not to marvel at its technical wizardry.

You could take out the clause between the commas and be left with a perfect sentence. But what extra information would be lost?

Focus on: Evaluating spoken presentations

As you have seen, a good review includes **information** and the reviewer's **opinion** (what he or she thinks about the film). Often, a range of **noun phrases** are used, with two or more adjectives to add information.

This **adjective** means 'they're the best'

...finest, computer-animated films...

This is the **noun** the adjectives are describing

This **adjective** informs us what sort of films they are

9 a) Describe to a partner in two to three minutes the plot of a film or TV programme you have seen recently. Make sure the basic features of reviews are included:

- the plot
- your opinion
- the main characters
- noun phrases to add detail.

For example:

> **Friend:** So, what's this new film like then?
>
> **You:** Well, it starts with… And it stars Colin Farrell as this down-and-out cop.

Use the table below for ideas (you can mix and match most combinations, as shown).

Start	Adjective 1	Adjective 2	Noun
He plays a/an… She plays a/an…	muscular	elegant	waitress
	amazing	rude	detective
	lonely	young	footballer
	shy	**nervous**	child
	quiet	emotional	**secret agent**

Add as many of your own ideas as you wish (talk about the story in the same way as the reviewers do).

b) When you have finished, ask your friend how well you described the programme or film, referring to the main features of reviews.

S&L19

Key Writing

S17

10 Write a three-paragraph review of your film or TV programme.

- Your paragraphs should give some **information** about the story or characters, and also suggest **what you think** of them.

- Try to use **noun phrases** like the ones you have practised.

- Use the **present tense**.

You may like to use this plan to help you:

> Paragraph 1: Give a quick overview of the story/plot. Make some sort of link or contrast with other programmes or previous films.

> Paragraph 2: Say something a bit more detailed about the story, the characters and where it takes place.

> Paragraph 3: Finish with a summary statement about the programme or film and what you think of it.

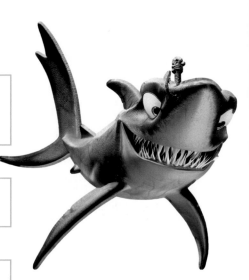

Exploring further

11 Extend these two descriptions between the commas to add a clause or phrase.

> It takes place in a dingy, dirty street, **close to**…, and stars Leigh Scotsville. Leigh finds himself being chased by a villain called Mugsy, **who**…, and gets locked up in his house for a week.

Once you have done this, see if you can redraft your three paragraphs to add further details in this way.

④ Unit 5 Assignment: TV reviewer

📺 Assessment Focuses

▶ AF4 Construct paragraphs and use cohesion within and between paragraphs
▶ AF7 Select appropriate and effective vocabulary

> **You:** write reviews of television programmes for a national magazine called *Top TV*. It lists the programmes for all channels, and has reviews (or previews) of the week's programmes.
>
> **Your task:** to write a review of an upcoming episode of the soap opera *EastEnders*.

Stage 1

You have watched the episode. Read through the notes you made.

Where: Set in Walford, East London. Mostly based around Albert Square, at the centre of town. Various other locations, including the Queen Vic pub and Bridge Street market.

Who: The Mitchells: mother Peggy, sons Phil and Grant, and daughter Sam. They own a number of businesses in Walford, including the Queen Vic pub.
The Fowlers: mother Pauline, son Martin and Martin's wife Sonya. They own a fruit stall on Bridge Street market.
The Beales: father Ian, children Lucy, Peter and Bobby. Ian owns the chip shop and café.
The Moons: Alfie, his wife Kat, his brother Spencer and their grandmother Nana Moon. They run the Queen Vic for the Mitchells.

Dot Branning – long-time resident of Walford. Works at the laundrette and is best friends with Pauline Fowler.

Lynne and Garry Hobbes – Kat Moon's sister and her husband. They are expecting their first child.

Billy Mitchell – disaster-prone cousin of the Mitchell family. Works as an odd job man for Sam Mitchell's gangster boyfriend, Andy Hunter.

Main storyline: Fairground ride collapses during Bridge Street fair – many people injured. Lynne cannot feel her baby and is rushed to hospital. Ian is hurt beneath rubble but worries about Peter and Lucy's safety. Dot and Pauline are trapped together and they argue. Spencer's leg is mangled; Kat comforts him until an ambulance arrives. Kat finds out Alfie has left Walford, but when Alfie hears of the disaster he races back to the Square. Billy loses his coat when he gives it to an injured boy. Andy is furious with him – the package he was carrying contained thousands of pounds!

Stage 2

Decide what **opinion** you have of the episode – was it good or bad? Now write down at least *five* key adjectives you might use in your review:

Good		Bad	
believable	pacy	unbelievable	slow
interesting	clever	boring	silly, stupid
moving	funny	cold (as in 'leaving you cold')	unfunny
watchable	dramatic	unwatchable	dull
exciting		unexciting	

Stage 3

Now write five descriptions of main characters, using the **adjective + noun** structure (see page 111 for help). For example:

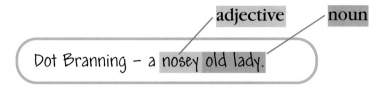

adjective   noun

Dot Branning – a nosey old lady.

Stage 4

Now draft your review. Use your notes and the plan below to help you. Remember to use an informal and friendly tone and to write in the present tense.

Paragraph 1: Introduce the programme and set the scene. (Remember, this is an unusual episode.)	*Tonight, another episode of EastEnders hits our screens. The action takes place at the Bridge Street fair…*
Paragraph 2: Write about the main storyline, including descriptions of the characters who play a key part.	*In this episode we learn that a fairground ride has collapsed and Dot Branning, one of the longest-surviving characters and a nosey old lady to the last, has been trapped…*
Paragraph 3: Mention the plot strands left unresolved and the final 'cliffhanger'.	*Meanwhile, Lynne has been rushed to hospital…*
The final paragraph: Write about your opinion of the episode.	*This episode of EastEnders has us…*

Challenge

Try writing an **alternative** last paragraph. In it, take the **opposite** point of view. For example, if you said you liked the episode in your first review, write about hating it in the second.

Unit 6 Far from home

① If a snake bites…

Aims

▸ Read a text telling you how to deal with a snake bite

▸ Explore how instructions are written (S13d)

▸ Think about how to compare the way people do things (W18)

▸ Give a set of simple instructions to guide a plane (S&L4)

The following text comes from a leaflet. The leaflet is aimed at children visiting Australia.

What to do for snake bites

If a snake bites you or your friend, then you will need to know what to do.

Be prepared

● Make sure that you carry a roll of **crepe bandage** with you when you go for a walk through the bush or long grass.

● Taking a **mobile phone** can also be very useful, as you can call for help if you need it.

5

First aid

- Do not wash the bite area. If there is some venom on the skin, this can help doctors find out which snake caused the bite, so that they can give some anti-venom to help fight the effect of the snake poison.
- Wrap a bandage firmly around the place where the bite is. (This should not be so tight that the blood supply is cut off. If the bandage hurts, it is too tight.)
- If the bite is on an arm or leg, wrap another bandage over as much of the limb as possible.
- Stop the person from using the arm or leg by putting on a splint (this can be a long stick).
- **Keep the injured person still**.
- Try to keep the person calm. Poison spreads more quickly if the heart beats faster.

Some things not to do

- Do not wait to see if the bite causes any problems. Always treat it straight away.
- Do not cut, wash or suck the bite. (Ignore all those old cowboy movies where the hero sucked out the poison!)
- Do not use ice on the bite. It will not be helpful.

Take action

- **Get help**. The faster the better.
- If there are at least two other people, you could try to carry the person to where help is, but don't make the bitten person walk.

Did you know?

- *Many Australian snakes are poisonous.*
- *Snakes in Australia are protected and should be left alone.*
- *A snake can 'unhinge' its jaws so that it can eat something 2 or 3 times the size of its own head.*
- *A snake changes its skin many times during the year. As it loses the old one a new coat is already underneath. (Wouldn't it be interesting if we could get new clothes like that? What sort of clothes would you grow?)*

Dr Kim says:
'Keep away from things that bite, like snakes and spiders. It's a good idea to be noisy when you are walking in the bush because snakes are shy and will go away if they hear you.'

117

Key Reading

Instruction texts

This is an **instruction** text. Its **purpose** is to tell someone clearly how to do something.

The main features of an instruction text are:

● It has a **clear design**, with a **step-by-step** approach often supported by **pictures** or **diagrams**. For example, the bullet points show where each instruction begins.

● It uses **imperative** verbs. These are verbs that tell (or **command**) you to do something, for example, '*Get* help.'

● It is written in a **plain and simple** style. You need to be able to understand the instructions and follow them easily, for example, 'Try to keep the person calm.'

● It is written in **chronological order**, often using **time connectives**, for example, 'when', 'first'.

S13d

1 How does the design of the leaflet support the step-by-step approach of an instruction text? Find at least two examples.

2 Find at least three examples of imperative verbs.

3 Another way of addressing the reader directly is to use the pronoun 'you'.

   a) Find two places where the word 'you' is used.

   b) What effect does this 'direct address' have?

4 a) Find three different ways in which the writer has used a plain and simple style in the leaflet.

   b) Why is it important that the verbs are easy to understand?

5 This leaflet does *not* use any time connectives, though some instruction texts do. How does it make the sequence clear without them?

Grammar for reading

Direct address is the term used when the writer speaks directly to the reader, using the word 'you'.

Purpose

6 The main purpose of this leaflet is to give instructions. However, it also includes some information and some advice.

    a) Identify where the information and advice sections are.

    b) How does the design help to distinguish these parts of the leaflet?

    c) Is there any information or advice elsewhere in the leaflet?

    d) Rewrite Dr Kim's words so that the advice becomes more like typical instruction, and the instruction becomes more like typical advice.

In emergencies, instructions must get to the point quickly. One way they do this is to use **imperatives**. It helps even more if the imperative starts the sentence:

> *Wrap* a bandage firmly around the place where the bite is.

This is much more effective than a general statement like this:

> It is a good idea to wrap a bandage firmly ...

Such a statement is more suited to an advice text.

7 a) Read the following sentences and reword them so that they become short, snappy instructions.

- If you don't want to be burnt, you shouldn't stay out in the sun for long periods.
- Extra care is needed when you visit hot countries like Australia.

    b) Now write two 'advice' style sentences for a partner to rewrite as instructions.

8 A text will only serve its purpose well if it is suited to its audience. Discuss with your partner how the writer of this leaflet aims it at their audience, and how successful the result is.

Reading for meaning

9 Sometimes reasons are given for the instructions, for example, 'Taking a mobile phone can also be very useful, as you can call for help if you need it.' Find two other places where reasons are given. Why are reasons given at these points?

10 Instruction texts are generally written in the present tense, for example, 'If the bite is on an arm or leg…'. However, in the 'Some things not to do' section, a past tense and a future tense are also used. Find these and explain why they have been used.

11 The writer has used quite a few brackets. Sometimes the full stop is inside the brackets, and sometimes it is outside. Identify an example of each and explain why the punctuation differs.

12 The writer has organised the 'Some things not to do' section so that it is particularly clear and easy to read. Each bullet point consists of an important command, then a second sentence.

a) What is the purpose of the second sentence in each case?

b) Write 'Some things not to do' for a leaflet on air travel aimed at children. Follow the same format, and include two sentences for each bullet point.

Exploring further: Connectives of time

Instead of using so many bullet points, this leaflet could have used connectives of time, such as 'first', 'then', 'when' to make it clear in what order you do things.

13 Rewrite the 'First aid' section using time connectives rather than bullet points. Discuss with a partner which version is more effective.

Focus on: Comparative adverbs

Sometimes you need to compare two ways of doing something. You can then use a **comparative adverb**. Look at these sentences:

> Poison spreads quickly.

Simple adverb describing how the poison spreads

> Poison spreads more quickly if the heart beats faster.

Comparative adverb comparing how quickly the poison spreads when the heart beats faster, with how quickly it spreads normally

To make a comparative adverb, you add the word 'more' in front of it.

 14 Rewrite each sentence below using a comparative adverb. You will have to compare the action with something else, by adding a phrase or clause beginning 'than', 'if' or 'when'.

- Jack spoke quietly.
- Karen crossed the road carefully.
- The car runs smoothly.

Exploring further: Irregular adverbs

A few common adverbs do not add 'more' to make the comparative:

- 'Fast' becomes 'faster', for example, 'The heart beats *faster* when you run.'
- 'Well' becomes 'better', for example, 'The second attempt worked *better* than the first.'

15 Write one sentence which includes the comparative adverb 'faster' and one which includes the comparative adverb 'better'.

Key Speaking and Listening

S&L4

16 In groups of three, you are going to work on giving spoken instructions.

- One of you is *an air traffic controller*. Your task is to give clear spoken instructions to the pilot, as the plane's computer has failed.

- One of you is an *air pilot*. You do exactly what you are told by the air traffic controller.

- One of you is an *observer*. You must point out when the pilot is not following the instructions exactly. You can also suggest how the air traffic controller can improve their instructions.

You will each have a turn as the air traffic controller. Your job is to guide the pilot to a destination you have chosen, or which your teacher has given you, using the map below and without naming any country.

For example: Travel east for 200 miles.
Slow down as we are close to the destination.

Discovering Brazil

Aims

▶ Read three information texts on Brazil

▶ Explore how information texts are written (S13a)

▶ Think about the effect of putting nouns at the beginning of sentences

▶ Explore how the language of texts on the same subject varies in formality (S15)

▶ Compare and contrast the way information is presented (R3)

▶ Rewrite an information text in a different way

The following texts give you information about Brazil. Text 1 is from a website, Text 2 is from a children's encyclopaedia and Text 3 is from a travel guide.

Text 1

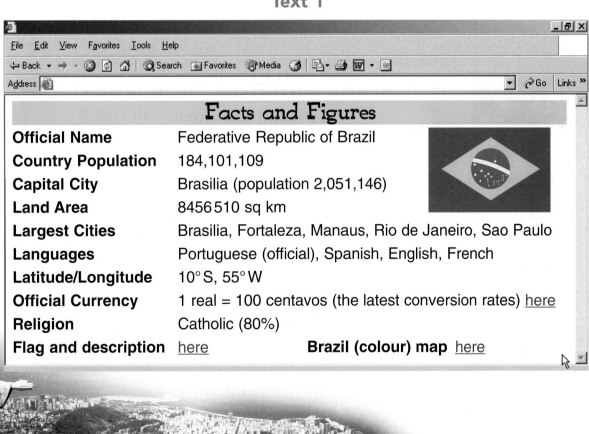

File Edit View Favorites Tools Help

⇐ Back ▾ ⇒ ▾ ⊗ 🗋 🏠 | 🔍 Search 📑 Favorites 📷 Media 🎯 | 🖅 ▾ 🖨 🕮 ▾ 🗐

Address 🗎 | ▾ 🔗 Go Links »

Facts and Figures

Official Name	Federative Republic of Brazil
Country Population	184,101,109
Capital City	Brasilia (population 2,051,146)
Land Area	8 456 510 sq km
Largest Cities	Brasilia, Fortaleza, Manaus, Rio de Janeiro, Sao Paulo
Languages	Portuguese (official), Spanish, English, French
Latitude/Longitude	10°S, 55°W
Official Currency	1 real = 100 centavos (the latest conversion rates) here
Religion	Catholic (80%)

Flag and description here   **Brazil (colour) map** here

Text 2

Brazil

Brazil is the largest country in South America. This huge territory covers nearly half the continent; it is almost as big as the USA. In the west are the foothills of the massive Andes mountains. To the east lie the beautiful beaches on the coast of the vast Atlantic ocean. However, even though it is a large country, a lot of Brazil is hard to access. The north-eastern corner of the country is dry and made up mostly of thorny scrub. The Amazon basin also has a very small population. Most Brazilians live in the cities – the three biggest cities are Sao Paolo, Brasilia (the capital) and beautiful Rio de Janeiro. Rio is famous for its colourful annual carnival. Brazilians are a vibrant mixture of races and cultures and this is reflected in their music, dance and art.

Brazil is one of the biggest producers of coffee in the world. Another important export is citrus fruit. Cattle, pigs and sheep are the most common livestock and there are also large deposits of iron ore and other minerals. Brazil is one of the ten biggest industrial nations in the world, but millions of people are poor, while only a few are very wealthy.

The national sport in Brazil is football (or *futebol* as Brazilians call it). They are the only nation to have won the World Cup four times (1958, 1962, 1970 and 1994) and are known to play the most creative and exciting style of the game. Brazilians are passionate about football – it is played all year round, and on big international game days, no one goes to work. Brazil's most famous player is Pelé, who retired in 1977. He scored over 1,000 goals in his 22-year career, and is known in Brazil as O Rei (the king).

5

10

15

20

25

30

35

Text 3

Brazil

Brazil's population is clustered along the Atlantic coast, and much of the country, including the massive Amazon Basin, remains scarcely populated and hard to access.

For most, the Brazilian journey begins in Rio de Janiero. For some it goes no farther. One of the world's great cities, Rio has developed a highly advanced culture of pleasure. It revolves around the famous beaches of Copacabana and Ipanema, and is fuelled by the music and dance of samba, the beauty of Corcovado and Pão de Açúcar (Sugar Loaf Mountain), the athleticism of soccer, the delight of an ice-cold *cerveja* (beer), the camaraderie of *papo* (chitchat) and the cult of the body beautiful. This hedonism reaches its climax every February or March, during the big bang that is Carneval – five days of revelry, unrivalled by any other party on the globe.

Rio de Janeiro state is blessed with some of the country's best beaches: from the world-renowned Búzios to the undeveloped Ilha Grande. Inland, the coastal mountains rise rapidly from lush, green, tropical forest, culminating in spectacular peaks. The mountains are punctuated by colonial cities and national parks where you can enjoy Brazil's best hiking and climbing.

The Amazon jungles are the world's largest tropical rainforest, fed by the world's largest river, and home to the richest and most diverse ecosystem on earth – a nature lover's ultimate fantasy! Though threatened by rapid deforestation, Brazilian Amazonia still offers years of exploration for the adventurous traveller.

Key Reading

Information texts

These texts are **information** texts. Their **purpose** is to present information on a subject in a clear and/or interesting way.

The main features of information texts are:

● They have **clear organisation**. Important or general information is often given first. The information is arranged in paragraphs or separate sections. For example, the third paragraph of Text 2 is all about football.

● Verbs are in the **present tense**. Information texts describe how things *are*. For example, in Text 2 it says: 'Brazil *is* the largest country in South America'.

● They use **factual writing**. The language is clear and precise. Technical terms or specialist words are often used. For example, in Text 2 it says: 'There are also large *deposits of iron ore and other minerals*.'

● The language is **formal**. Information texts are written in Standard English and pay close attention to the conventions of grammar. For example, in Text 3 it says: 'Rio has developed a highly advanced culture of pleasure.'

S13a

1 Find evidence for all four of these features in the three texts.

2 Why is Text 2 organised into three paragraphs?

3 If Text 1 were written to include verbs, what tense would they be in? Rephrase one piece of information to include a verb, and check your answer.

4 Text 3 contains some technical terms that are used in Geography. Imagine that you are adding a glossary to the entry so that Year 5 students can understand it. How would you define these terms:

a) tropical rainforest

b) ecosystem

c) deforestation?

Purpose

The purpose of an information text is **to describe the way things are**. Most texts do this in a clear and straightforward way. This is so that the reader:

● can find the information that he or she wants quickly

● understands it easily.

Often **nouns** are used to begin sentences. This is so the reader knows exactly what the sentence is going to be about. For example, in line 12 of Text 2 this sentence appears:

> **Rio** is famous for its colourful annual carnival.

The **noun** 'Rio' tells you what this sentence is going to be about

In line 1 a **noun phrase** does the same job:

The **noun phrase** 'this huge territory' tells you this sentence is going to be about Brazil

> **This huge territory** covers nearly half the continent; **it** is almost as big as the USA.

The **pronoun** 'it' refers to Brazil. It tells you that the next part of the sentence is still about the country

5 Look at the last two sentences in this paragraph. How has the writer made the subject clear? Use the terms 'noun', 'noun phrase' and 'pronoun' in your answer.

For variety, more elaborate writing can put the subject later in the sentence. A **participle phrase** that agrees with the subject comes first. Look at this example from Text 3:

> Though **threatened** by rapid deforestation, Brazilian Amazonia still offers years of exploration for the adventurous traveller.

A **participle phrase** begins the sentence. It agrees with the noun that follows. Note the comma at the end of the clause

A **noun phrase** tells you this sentence is going to be about the Amazon region

6 Rewrite these two short sentences as one complex sentence. The sentence will start with a **participle phrase**.

- The Rio Carneval excites the imagination of the traveller.
- The Rio Carneval takes place over five days in February or March.

Grammar for reading

A **noun** is a word that names something. Often a group of words does the same job, for example, 'The deep-sea divers'. This is called a **noun phrase**.

A **participle** is a form of the verb that allows it to be used as an adjective. Present participles end in '-ing', for example, 'flying', 'sailing'. Past participles usually end in '-ed', for example, 'defeated', 'connected'.

Reading for meaning

7 What features of Text 1 are only found on web pages?

8 In Text 2, how does the writer organise his material to give the reader a 'tour' of the country in paragraphs 1 and 2? Look closely at sentences 3 and 4.

9 If information texts only used plain and straightforward language they would lose the interest of their audience. Text 2 sometimes uses powerful or descriptive adjectives or verbs for this reason, such as 'the beautiful beaches on the coast of the vast Atlantic ocean' in line 5. Find two or three more examples and say what the effect is of each one.

10 In Text 3, what is the effect of the flowery phrases 'highly advanced culture of pleasure', 'pristine tropical beaches' and 'fuelled by the music and dance of samba'? Where else might you find such language? Rewrite two of these phrases so that they are more suitable for an encyclopaedia.

R3 **Focus on:** Presenting the information

Information can be presented in many different ways. Usually this depends on the exact purpose of the text.

11 In groups, compare and contrast the three information texts on Brazil. Draw up and complete a chart like the one below. Include any thoughts that you have on the **effect** of each feature.

Design/layout	Web page	Encyclopaedia entry	Travel guide
Use of bold/italic and colour	Bold used to show the subheadings – simple but clear. Colour to mark the main headings and the hyperlinks – makes them stand out.	Bold used for title only. Could do with some more bold to highlight main words?	

You should cover the following features of design/layout:

- Use of bold/italic and colour
- The size and style of the typeface
- The illustrations
- Headings and subheadings

You should cover the following features of language/style:

- Length of sentences
- Use of paragraphs
- Style of writing - plain or descriptive?
- Are facts or opinions given?
- Formality of the writing.

12 Finally, think about the exact purpose of each text. Does this explain the differences in the table? Be prepared to present your table to the class.

Key Writing

13 Your task is to rewrite the information in Text 3 so that it could be included in a children's encyclopaedia.

Remember to:

- use formal language
- use sub-headings to divide up text
- keep your 8–12 year-old audience in mind.

You could begin like this:

The population of Brazil is concentrated on the Atlantic coast. Much of the country, including the Amazon Basin, is hardly populated and is difficult to reach.

3 Bournemouth in the rain

Aims

- Read a traveller's tale about a rainy visit (R6)
- Explore how recount texts are written and structured (S13b)
- Analyse how paragraphs are used to mark a change of focus (S8)
- Explore how imagery can be used to create vivid description
- Imagine how the tale continues, and write the next episode

The American writer and humorist Bill Bryson lived in Britain from 1973 to 1995. This is an extract from his account of a trip he took before he left.

Bournemouth in the rain

And so to Bournemouth. I arrived at five-thirty in the evening in a driving rain. Night had fallen heavily and the streets were full of swishing cars, their headlights sweeping through bullets of shiny rain. I'd lived in Bournemouth for two years and thought I knew it reasonably well, but the area around the station had been extensively rebuilt, with new roads and office blocks and one of those befuddling networks of pedestrian subways that force you to surface every few minutes like a gopher to see where you are.

By the time I reached the East Cliff, a neighbourhood of medium-sized hotels perched high above a black sea, I was soaked through and muttering. The one thing to be said for Bournemouth is that you are certainly spoiled for choice with hotels. Among the many gleaming palaces of comfort that lined every street for blocks around, I selected an establishment on a side-street for no reason other than I rather liked its sign: neat capitals in pink neon glowing through the slicing rain. I stepped inside, shedding water, and could see at a glance it was a good choice – clean, nicely old-fashioned, attractively priced, and with the kind of warmth that makes your glasses steam and brings on sneezing fits. I decanted several ounces of water from my sleeve and asked for a single room for two nights.

'Is it raining out?' the reception girl asked brightly as I filled in the registration card between sneezes and pauses to wipe water from my face with the back of my arm.

'No, my ship sank and I had to swim the last seven miles.'

25 'Oh, yes?' she went on in a manner that made me suspect she was not attending to my words closely. 'And will you be dining with us tonight, Mr –' she glanced at my water-smeared card '– Mr Brylcreem?' I considered the alternative – a long slog through stair-rods of rain – and felt inclined to stay in. Besides, between her cheerily bean-sized brain and my smeared 30 scrawl, there was every chance they would charge the meal to another room. I said I'd eat in, accepted a key and drippingly found my way to my room.

Among the many hundreds of things that have come a long way in Britain since 1973, few have come further than the average English hostelry. Nowadays you get a colour TV, coffee-making tray with a little 35 packet of modestly tasty biscuits, a private bath with fluffy towels, a little basket of cotton-wool balls in rainbow colours, and an array of sachets or little plastic bottles of shampoo, bath gel and moisturizing lotion. My room even had an adequate bedside light and two soft pillows. I was very happy. I ran a deep bath, emptied into it all the gels and moisturizing creams 40 (don't be alarmed; I've studied this closely and can assure you that they are all the same substance), and, as a fiesta of airy bubbles began their slow ascent towards a position some three feet above the top of the bath, returned to the room and slipped easily into the self-absorbed habits of the lone traveller, unpacking my rucksack with deliberative care, draping wet 45 clothes over the radiator, laying out clean ones on the bed with as much fastidiousness as if I were about to go to my first high-school prom, arranging a travel clock and reading material with exacting precision on the bedside table, adjusting the lighting to a level of considered cosiness, and finally retiring, in perky spirits and with a good book, for a long wallow in 50 the sort of luxuriant foam seldom seen outside of Joan Collins movies.

Key Reading

Recount texts

This text is a **recount**. Its **purpose** is to recount or tell the reader about a series of events.

The main features of a recount text are:

- It is mainly told in the **past tense**, for example, 'I *arrived* at five-thirty in the evening…'.

- It describes events in **time order** and uses **connectives of time**, for example, '*By the time* I reached the East Cliff…'.

- It uses **paragraphs** to mark a change of focus, for example, 'And so to Bournemouth'.

- It uses **descriptive language** to bring the events alive, such as adjectives, powerful verbs and imagery, for example, 'a fiesta of airy bubbles began their slow ascent'.

S13b

1 Find examples of all four of these features in the text.

2 The past tense is not always used in this recount. Find some verbs in the present and future tenses and explain why they have been used.

3 Where in the extract does Bryson change his focus to just one part of Bournemouth? How does he signal this to the reader?

4 How does the last sentence of the extract use descriptive writing to good effect?

Purpose

Both narrative and recount texts aim to tell a story. The difference between these two text types is that narrative relates to fiction, recount to fact.

5 a) What features of narrative texts does this extract show? (Refer to page 72 for a reminder of these.)

b) How true do you think this recount text actually is?

6 a) Identify the different sources of humour that help make this recount entertaining. With a partner, discuss which you think is the funniest and why.

b) Is Bryson's main purpose in this extract to be funny? If not, what else is he aiming to do?

. . . .

Reading for meaning

> **dialogue** a conversation between two people. This can be spoken or written down.

R6

7 How effectively does Bill Bryson set the scene in the first three sentences of the extract?

8 The short passage of dialogue is carefully written.

a) 'No, my ship sank and I had to swim the last seven miles' (line 24), has no indication of the speaker. Why not?

b) What is the effect of breaking the receptionist's final question with the words 'she glanced at my water-smeared card' (line 27)?

9 Write notes on the following aspects of the final paragraph:

a) the length of the sentences

b) lists

c) the precise and detailed use of language.

10 There are lots of references to rain, water and wetness in this passage.

a) Make a table of all the words or phrases that refer to water.

b) Which is the best word or phrase, in your opinion?

c) How effectively does Bryson use water as a motif in this extract?

> **motif** a theme that recurs in a piece of writing, art or music, to create a kind of pattern

Exploring further: Imagery

Bill Bryson creates vivid images or pictures by using metaphors and similes. A **metaphor** is a particular kind of image which describes one thing as something else. The image created gives extra impact to the writing. For example:

> The streets were full of swishing cars, their headlights sweeping through **bullets** of **shiny rain**.

'Bullets' is a metaphor, as the word is usually linked with guns. It suggests the rain is coming hard and fast, and hurting. 'Shiny' adds detail to the image

'Rain' is the subject of the description

11 Look at lines 10–11 and line 13.

For both examples identify:

- what the subject of the description is
- what the metaphor is (what new image is being used)
- what impact the metaphor adds to the description.

12 Identify the simile in the first paragraph and evaluate what effect it has.

Focus on: Structuring a recount text

A recount text describes a series of events. These events can be plotted on a **timeline**. A timeline is not only a useful way of noting the main events in a recount text, it is also a good tool for planning your own recounts.

13 Construct a timeline for 'Bournemouth in the rain'. Include at least eight of the most important events.

S4 **14** Look at the verbs in the following phrases:

a) 'Night *had fallen* heavily' (line 2)

b) 'I *had lived* in Bournemouth for two years' (line 4)

c) 'The area around the station *had been* extensively *rebuilt*' (lines 5–6)

What tense are these verbs in? How could you mark these events on your timeline?

S8 **15** If an event in a recount deals with a different person, place or idea, it usually begins a new paragraph. Look back at the text.

a) What different focus has the writer given to each paragraph?

b) A **topic sentence** is the main sentence that shows the reader what a new paragraph is about. It is usually at the beginning of a paragraph. What is the topic sentence of each paragraph of this text?

c) Indicate the paragraph breaks on your timeline somehow. Does the paragraphing relate to the events on the timeline in any way?

· ·

Key Writing

16 Imagine you are Bill Bryson. Your task is to write three or four paragraphs describing what happened after (or during) your bath.

a) First of all, draw a timeline of events.

b) Then organise your material into paragraphs.

c) Finally, write your recount.

Remember:

● Imagine that you are Bill Bryson. So use 'I' and 'my' (the **first person**).

● Describe events as if they happened in the past. So put the events in **time order** and use the **past tense**.

● Make your recount **entertaining**. Include good descriptions, dialogue and/or humour.

④ Unit 6 Assignment: Travel guide to Greece

Assessment Focuses

▶ **AF3** Organise and present whole texts effectively, sequencing and structuring information, ideas and events

▶ **AF4** Construct paragraphs and use cohesion within and between paragraphs

---

You: are a travel writer.

Your task: to write an introduction for a travel guide to Greece.

Stage 1

Here are two pages of notes giving information about Greece. Unfortunately the notes have not been organised into topics. Four possible topics to be covered in the introduction are: 'Natural features', 'Tourist attractions', 'General information' and 'Planning your trip'.

Organise the notes into the four topics.

- seaside: lots of beaches and islands
- over 1400 islands
- location: in south-east Europe, on the Mediterranean Sea
- best time to visit: spring and autumn
- nearly 80% of country is mountains/hills
- area: 132,000 sq km
- get free maps from Greek National Tourist Organisation
- capital: Athens
- mostly mainland
- character: relaxed, child-loving
- take sturdy shoes and light clothing

- population: approximately 10,700,000
- climate: hot dry summers
- ancient sites and cities, like Knossos
- contact Greek National Tourist Organisation on 020 7495 9303
- main islands: Crete, Euboea, Rhodes, Chios, Corfu
- festivals with dancing, singing, feasting
- currency: euro
- official name: Hellenic Republic
- highest point in Greece: Mount Olympus (2917 m)
- travel insurance is a good idea

You may want to use a spidergram to organise these notes, like the one begun below:

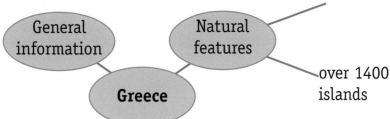

General information

Natural features

Greece

over 1400 islands

Stage 2

You are going to write one paragraph on each topic. First of all, decide which order you want the paragraphs to go in. Remember that the most important, or the most general, information goes first.

Stage 3

Finally, turn these notes into four clear paragraphs for your introduction to Greece. Remember to:

- use the **present tense**
- make your sentences clear and precise
- put the **noun** or **noun phrase** at the front to show the reader what your sentences are about
- use **topic sentences** to tell your reader what each paragraph is about
- use **formal language** but also powerful or **descriptive adjectives** and **verbs** at times: this is part of a travel guide, not an encyclopaedia entry
- add some **design features** to make your introduction attractive and easy to follow. For example, you could include **subheadings**, add some **illustrations** and experiment with **different sizes** or **colours of font**.

 Words and pictures

 Aims

▶ Look at three adverts and explore how they persuade the reader (S13e)

▶ Think about how important the pictures and design are in adverts (R11)

▶ Analyse the ways that words can be persuasive in adverts, and explore how slogans work (S&L8)

▶ Defend a point of view in a persuasive way (S&L5)

Look at the adverts on the following pages. This advert for VSO was displayed above the seats in London Underground trains.

> **Will you remember today forever?** You went to work. The tube was strangely empty. You got a hilarious email. Someone made you a perfect cup of tea. You ate a delicious sandwich. The photocopier did not jam. There were no delays on the tube home. But will you remember today forever? You saw an ad on the tube that changed your life. You decided to do something about the state of the world. You offered your professional experience to VSO. You volunteered to share your skills in the world's poorest communities. You stood up not because there were no seats, but to be counted. To say you wanted to make a difference. This is your chance. This is the ad. This is the website: www.vso.org.uk. This is the number: 020 8780 7500. This is the day.
>
> **VSO**
> Sharing skills
> Changing lives
> Registered Charity Number 313757

The following advert appears in a tourist brochure for Blackpool.

This advert is for Wall's Carte D'Or ice cream.

Key Reading

> ## Persuasion texts
>
> These are **persuasion** texts. Their **purpose** is to persuade the reader to do something.
>
> The main features of persuasion texts are:
>
> - They include a **series of points**, in a **logical order**, supporting a single viewpoint, for example, 'Blackpool Sea Life Centre…is a watery world of all things marine.'
> - They use **visual images** or **sound** to grab the interest of the audience, for example, the main image in the ice cream advert.
> - They use **colourful** and **suggestive** language, for example, '…sh-sh-shudder as sharks pass within inches'.
> - They include **personal** language, including direct address (use of first or second person), for example, 'Will you remember today forever?'

S13e

1 How does the Wall's advert make a 'series of points'?

2 How important is design in each of these adverts, compared with the text?

3 Which is the most effective word in the Wall's advert? Can you say why?

4 The language of the VSO advert is deliberately not colourful (for example, 'You went to work'). So how does the language create a powerful effect?

5 The Sea Life Centre advert uses the slogan '20,000 leagues ahead of the rest!' How effective is this slogan? Give your reasons.

6 Why does the VSO advert use so much direct address and personal language?

Purpose

7 The Sea Life Centre advert gives you a lot of information.

a) Find three important pieces of information that it gives the reader.

b) Is giving information the main purpose of the advert?

8 Look at the Wall's advert. What is its main purpose?

9 The VSO advert does not seem to be selling anything – or is it?

Reading for meaning

'Reading' an advert means far more than looking at the words. The design of the advert is very important too – especially its pictures.

The design of the Wall's advert has been analysed below:

colour scheme:
● bold colours
● mostly red and white, but green of nuts also used
● colours of design match colours of ice cream

main text:
● large clear capitals
● takes up top third of page
● shaped around the image

main image:
● large and clear
● in centre of page
● set at an angle
● shows product name on side

border:
● gives advert a clear frame
● makes whole page look like lid of an ice cream tub

other text:
● less important, so small and at bottom
● slogan in gold and slightly bigger

logo:
● tucked out of the way but not hidden – it pushes into picture area

R11

10 In pairs, discuss the other two adverts. Is their design effective? Talk about the following features:

● the images used (for example, subjects, colours, shapes, number)
● how the text is presented (for example, size, colour, variety)
● the overall design.

11 Collect four or five adverts from newspapers or magazines that you think have an effective design, and analyse them in the same way. Be ready to present your ideas.

Exploring further: Context

The **context** of an advert is where it will be displayed or broadcast (TV, billboard, magazine, radio) and its audience (who it is aimed at).

12 Advertisers have to take the context of the advert into account. Discuss:

a) how the designers of the VSO advert have taken its context into account

b) how you would adapt the Wall's advert so that it was suitable for radio.

Focus on: Colourful and suggestive words

Sometimes there are very few words in an advert. But every word will be carefully chosen to persuade you to buy something or do something.

There are many ways in which the words can be persuasive:

● They can **address the reader** directly, for example, using 'you' or commands.

● They can be **colourful or powerful**, for example, lively adjectives, or words that make a particular sound or suggest a sound effect.

● They can be **emotive or suggestive**, for example, they make you feel something, or they suggest a particular image or meaning.

Look at how the words in the Wall's advert persuade you in all of these ways:

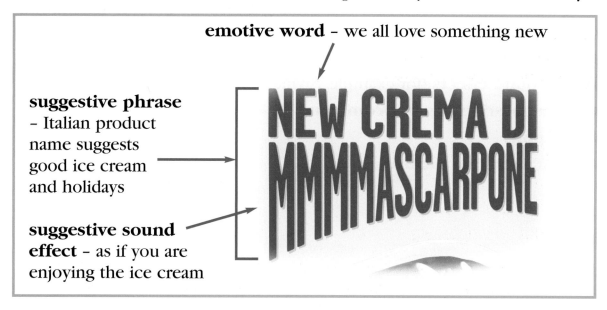

emotive word – we all love something new

suggestive phrase – Italian product name suggests good ice cream and holidays

suggestive sound effect – as if you are enjoying the ice cream

NEW CREMA DI MMMMASCARPONE

143

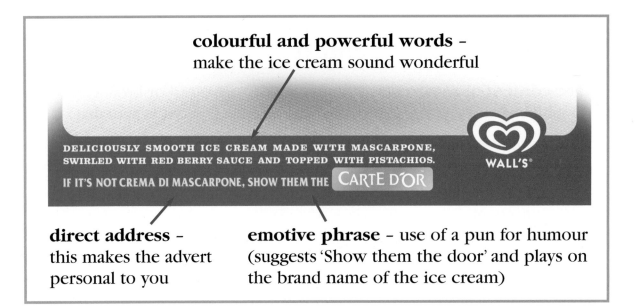

colourful and powerful words – make the ice cream sound wonderful

DELICIOUSLY SMOOTH ICE CREAM MADE WITH MASCARPONE, SWIRLED WITH RED BERRY SAUCE AND TOPPED WITH PISTACHIOS. IF IT'S NOT CREMA DI MASCARPONE, SHOW THEM THE CARTE D'OR

WALL'S®

direct address – this makes the advert personal to you

emotive phrase – use of a pun for humour (suggests 'Show them the door' and plays on the brand name of the ice cream)

S&L8

13 In groups, talk about the way words are used persuasively in the Sea Life Centre advert and the VSO advert. Then draw up a grid like the one below to record your findings.

Word/phrase	Type of persuasion used: • direct address • colourful/powerful words • emotive/suggestive words	What effect it has
All aboard	direct address suggestive phrase	Grabs reader from the start. The phrase also suggests you are about to go on a voyage.

Slogans

Slogans have to be memorable and striking if they are going to remind you of the product. Good slogans work in several different ways. They can:

● use a **strong rhythm**, including repetition

● use **sound effects** (for example, rhyme, alliteration)

● ask a **question** or give a **command**

● use **puns**

● paint a **striking picture**.

14 What methods do the following slogans use to make them memorable? Which is the most effective?

a) 'The future's bright – the future's Orange.' (Orange)

b) 'Just do it.' (Nike)

c) 'Let your fingers do the walking.' (Yellow Pages)

d) 'Takes a licking and keeps on ticking.' (Timex)

e) 'Running water for you.' (Thames Water).

Exploring further: Special sentences

A **special sentence** is one that does not have all of the ingredients of an ordinary sentence. Special sentences may lack a subject or a finite verb, for example, 'Relax', 'warning'.

15 The text of adverts often has unusual grammar, including the use of special (or minor) sentences.

a) Why do you think this is?

b) Find some examples of special sentences in the three adverts and discuss their effect.

Key Speaking and Listening

S&L5

16 In the same groups as for question 13, your task is to compare the three adverts and persuade the class that one is the best. You will need to:

● Give reasons or evidence for your statements, for example, 'The colours of the advert are effective *because they remind me of the sea.*'

● Speak in a persuasive way, for example, 'Don't you think the colours are just fantastic?'

● Refer to the context of the adverts, giving reasons why they are suited to their setting and audience. For example, 'The way the VSO advert speaks to the person sitting on the tube…'

Practise your presentation in groups.

The power of advertising

Aims

▶ Read a newspaper article that expresses a point of view about advertising

▶ Explore how argument texts are written

▶ Think about how sentences are organised into paragraphs (S10)

▶ Understand more about the passive, and practise using it (S5)

The following text is a column from *The Independent*. In the column, Lisa Markwell describes how even her young son, Peter, is affected by the power of advertising.

The advertising is working, damn it

Why is it that my son knows how much the latest Teenage Mutant Ninja Turtles playset costs, but doesn't know six times seven? Why does he suggest
5 that we have Wall's sausage balls for supper, but can't remember what he had for lunch? It is, of course, the power of advertising. He only watches television for about one hour on
10 Saturday morning, and one afternoon a week. But in those brief moments, he's wide-eyed (and wide-brained) to soak up the messages directed at him.

New research by Harris Interactive
15 shows that seven-year-olds are old enough to be a target consumer for youth market advertising. The idea is, apparently, get 'em young and then when they're old enough to spend, they
20 will be indoctrinated in the delights of, well, probably Sunny Delight.

What used to be an advertising frenzy in the weeks before Christmas doesn't seem to be abating as summer

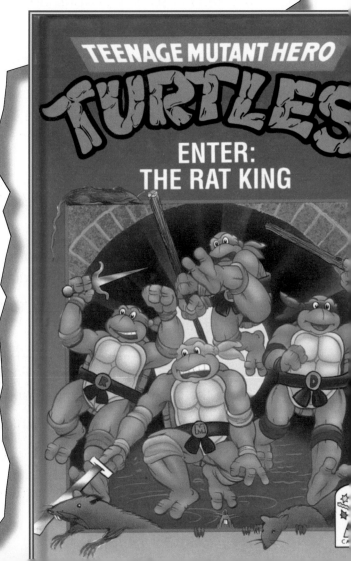

approaches. My son doesn't actually have any money to spend on junk food, plastic toys and identikit pop – he gets very little pocket money and is a careful saver. But that doesn't stop him remembering the consumer goodies.

On the subject of pocket money, the rules for parents are very ambiguous these days. When I was young we got a Jamboree bag of sweets on Saturday mornings and a few pennies every now and then for doing chores. Now it varies between £1 a week and £10 (and this is for seven- and eight-year-olds).

One child of my acquaintance gets the latter, plus 'loans' from his dad for new Playstation games. I'm not sure if that's a way of teaching the child economics or giving the father a way to play a wider variety of mindless games without incurring the wrath of his wife…

My doctor's son, prone to early

morning moods and 'won't go to school' antics, gets 50p for every morning that he's dressed and ready for school with all the necessary kit by the 8.30am deadline. So he makes a tidy profit and his mum keeps her sanity. Wise move.

In my house it's £1 a week basic, with extras for room tidying, helping at Sainsbury's and getting head teacher awards from school. Into the piggybank it goes until he wants something particular – like the latest vile Alien Baby to impress his mates in the playground.

Anyway, what really worries me, and my wallet, is that Peter and his class mates also spend a great deal of time poring over the Argos catalogue. Every Bionicle figure is noted; every Barbie accessory is studied. If only they took as much notice of their times tables.

But if I'm honest, I would have to say that their retail interest is a product of our times. We are all consumers now, whether of penny sweets or second homes. Last week, while on holiday, Peter sang the jingle for Kandoo lavatory wipes (the soundtrack to daring himself deeper into the sea – 'you can do it with Kandoo'). Then there was 'I shall eat a fishy on a little dishy' as we walked to a restaurant on the harbour.

But what really worried me was when he said: 'Mum, did you know that calls with Tele2 are only 2p, that's cheaper than BT?' No I didn't and I want to know more. The advertising is working, damn it.

Key Reading

Argument texts

This is an **argument** text. Its **purpose** is to express a point of view, and persuade the reader to agree with it.

The main features of an argument text are:

- It includes a **series of points**, in a **logical order**, for example, the third paragraph makes a point about the amount of advertising aimed at children through the year.

- The points are backed up by **evidence** or **reasons**, for example, 'New research by Harris Interactive shows…'

- It uses **formal** but **effective** language, for example, 'Every Bionicle figure is noted; every Barbie accessory is studied.'

- It has a **reasonable tone**, to win over the audience, for example, 'It is, of course, the power of advertising.'

1 The first two paragraphs of the article have been annotated below and on page 149 to show examples of all of these features. Make a note of examples of these features for the rest of the article.

two questions at the start – an effective opening that grabs the reader

Why is it that my son knows how much the latest Teenage Mutant Ninja Turtles playset costs, but doesn't know six times seven? Why does he suggest that we have Walls sausage balls for supper, but can't remember what he had for lunch? It is, of course, the power of advertising. He only watches television for about one hour on Saturday morning, and one afternoon a week. But in those brief moments, he's wide-eyed (and wide-brained) to soak up the messages directed at him.

effective use of language

reason given for the questions

formal language, a bit like a report

new point (about research) has a new paragraph. This also provides **evidence** for the main point in paragraph 1

New research by Harris Interactive shows that seven-year-olds are old enough to be a target consumer for youth market advertising. The idea is, apparently, get 'em young and then when they're old enough to spend, they will be indoctrinated in the delights of, well, probably Sunny Delight.

reasonable tone – 'apparently' suggests she doesn't know everything. Attempt at humour also to **win over audience**

Purpose

2 The purpose of an argument text is to win the audience over to your point of view. What is this writer's point of view? What is the main point that she is making?

The author wins the audience over to her view by backing up her points. There are four main ways that she does this:

● by giving **evidence** or **reasons** for her view

● by referring to her **own experience**

● by giving an **example** of what she is saying

● by going into her point in **greater detail**.

3 What evidence is given in paragraph 2 to back up the writer's view that advertising is powerful?

4 Find two other places in the article where she relates her own experience to back up her view.

5 What examples of the power of advertising does the writer give in paragraph 1?

6 What further detail does she add in paragraphs 5, 6 and 7 on the subject of pocket money?

Reading for meaning

7 The newspaper article is mostly written in formal language. However, there are some informal features, such as contracted words and a conversational style.

a) Identify the informal language in paragraph 2.

b) Why has the writer used informal language here and elsewhere in the article?

8 In line 32 the writer starts a separate discussion or digression about pocket money.

  a) How does she signal the start of this digression to the reader?

  b) Where does the digression end, and how does she signal this?

9 Why is the final paragraph an effective end to the article?

Grammar for reading

Conversational language is the language of speech rather than writing. It is more informal and includes **contracted words**, for example, 'Go and fetch 'im' instead of 'Go and fetch him' or 'He doesn't want to' instead of 'He does not want to'.

Focus on: Organising paragraphs

Effective writers, especially in argument texts, give each paragraph a main point and then back up that point in different ways in the rest of the paragraph. For example:

Main point: adverts are now targeting seven-year-olds

> New research by Harris Interactive shows that seven-year-olds are old enough to be a target consumer for youth market advertising. The idea is, apparently, get 'em young and then when they're old enough to spend, they will be indoctrinated in the delights of, well, probably Sunny Delight.

Other sentence: the reason for targeting seven-year-olds is to train them up to spend later

10 In pairs, find the main point of paragraph 3 (lines 22–31). Then work out how the rest of the paragraph supports that point. Remember that the other sentences in a paragraph can back up the main point in four different ways (see page 149).

11 Now, on your own, do the same for paragraphs 4, 5 and 6.

Exploring further: 'The former' and 'the latter'

In line 41, Lisa Markwell says, 'One child of my acquaintance gets the latter'. You can use 'the former' and 'the latter' to refer to the first (former) or second (latter) of two things that have just been mentioned. In this case, the previous sentence shows that the two things were pocket money of £1 a week (the former) and £10 a week (the latter).

12 Write a sentence using the terms 'former' and/or 'latter' to follow on from this one:

'The Nike advert was followed by an advert for cat food.'

Focus on: Using the passive

● In **active sentences**, the subject performs the action on the object.

● In **passive sentences**, the subject is on the receiving end of the action:

Active sentence

SUBJECT	VERB	OBJECT
The police	arrested	the burglar

Passive sentence

SUBJECT	VERB	AGENT ('BY' PHRASE)
The burglar	was arrested	by the police

Sometimes passive sentences have the effect of emphasising the thing being acted on, rather than the doer of the action (or agent).

13 Look at this sentence from the article, which is in the passive:

'Even her young son, Peter, is affected by the power of advertising.'

a) Write out the sentence and label the subject, the verb and the agent ('by' phrase).

b) Which of the following is being emphasised in the sentence: 'Even her young son, Peter' or 'the power of advertising'?

151

c) Now make the sentence active. What happens to the verb?

d) Which is the more powerful sentence?

Exploring further: The passive without an agent

The passive is often used without an agent ('by phrase'). This emphasises the subject and the action even more. For example, in the sentence 'The sides of the triangles were measured', we don't need to know who measured the triangles.

14 Look at this sentence (lines 69–70): 'Every Bionicle figure is noted; every Barbie accessory is studied.' What is the effect of using the passive here?

Key Writing

15 Write a two- or three-paragraph letter to the editor of *The Independent*, arguing either *for* or *against* Lisa Markwell's article on toy advertising.

a) Choose two or three points from the article (see the list below) to support or counter in your argument, or use your own notes from question 10.
  ● Children have detailed knowledge of products from adverts but their general knowledge is poor.
  ● Children are targeted by advertisers throughout the year from as young as seven years old.
  ● Parents sometimes offer too much pocket money, thus increasing children's power to buy.
  ● Children are only following adults, who are also influenced by advertising in what they buy.

b) Decide how you will organise your first paragraph. What will the opening sentence of your argument be? Will you use a question to catch the reader's attention? Or will you lead off with your first main point?

c) Give a reason or use an example from your own experience to back up your main point.

d) Use a reasonable tone and formal language, including the passive where appropriate.

e) Repeat b), c) and d) for your second and third paragraphs.

③ Pen pal dangers

Aims

▶ Read a magazine article advising you about pen pals

▶ Explore how advice texts are written (R10)

▶ Analyse two important features of informal language (R13)

▶ Write a piece of advice in a style that suits the audience (Wr17)

The following text comes from a teen magazine.

Pen Pal Dangers

Thought putting pen to paper was a harmless way of making a new mate? Maybe not – as mizz *discovers...*

Having a pen pal is a fantastic way to make new mates from different places. By meeting through official school schemes or exchanges where teachers can make sure everything is above

5 board, pen pals can become friends for life. But the fact is, meeting someone via an internet club or through a magazine does have risks.

10 Take meeting someone creepy online. It's awful, but you can log off quick sharp. If you've written letters to them, however, that person's got

15 your address, as well as loads of info about you that you've let them in on. It'd be like texting summat really personal to your best mate,

20 then realising someone else had read it instead. So make sure that you get sussed before you start scribbling...

Louisa's story

25 *Reader Louisa, 13, was in a pen pal ad last year. She recently found out her new mate, Nick, was actually a 46-year-old man…*

"I was really chuffed when a mag sent me 60 letters from people wanting to be my pen pal. I wrote back to all of them but, after a bit,
30 started writing regularly to Nick. He said that he was 14 and at boarding school in Cornwall.

"It was exciting that a lad was writing to me and I'd take his letters to school and read them with my mates. He never mentioned his friends but I just thought he was a bit of a loner.

"Then, a few months ago, he sent me a letter mentioning sex. I was
35 so shocked, I wrote and told him I didn't want to be his pen pal any more. Not long after, we got a phone call. It was his dad, explaining that Nick was actually 46 years old and had mental health problems.

"At first I was really frightened cos he knew where I lived and I made my mates stick to me like glue at school. I feel okay now, though – the
40 police say Nick lives in a hospital, which means he can't come here.

"None of my family realised what was happening, but who'd have thought writing letters could be so dangerous?"

Pen pal pointers

First off, don't panic and ring up your pen pal to accuse them of
45 being an impostor. Nearly all people who write'll be genuine, but it's important to follow *mizz's* safety tips:

- You might get over 100 replies but don't try to juggle too many. Go through 'em with your folks and pick a couple you'd like to be friends with.
50 - Take your pen pal friendship slowly. There's no need to tell them every little fact about yourself until you know them properly.
- Don't ever give out your address or phone number without checking with your parents first. The best thing to do is get
55 your folks to call the parents of your future pen pal to check everything's cool.
- Make sure that you tell your parents immediately if you read something that makes you feel uncomfortable. You can then tackle the problem together.

60 And remember – as a *mizz* pen pal, we don't give your address out to any old bod with a fancy stationery set. No personal details appear in the mag. We send you details of your wannabe pen pals and you pick who you want to write to.

Key Reading

Advice texts

This is an **advice** text. Its **purpose** is to advise the reader to do (or not to do) something.

The main features of an advice text are:

● It includes a **series of points** in a **logical order**, for example, 'First off, don't panic and ring up your pen pal to accuse them of being an impostor.'

● Its **design** helps to make the structure of the advice clear, for example, the safety tips are written as bullet points.

● It uses **direct address**, with commands to the reader or the words 'you' or 'your', for example, 'It's awful, but you can log off quick sharp.'

● It has a **conversational** or **informal** tone, for example, 'So make sure that you get sussed before you start scribbling…'

R10

1 Read through the first and last sections of this article and find evidence for each of these features of advice texts.

2 What point is the writer making in the first paragraph (lines 3–9)? Is it logical to make this point here?

3 The first paragraph is written in an impersonal way – there is no reference to 'you'. Can you explain why the writer has done this?

4 What design features make this an effective advice text?

5 Find all the examples of direct address in paragraph 2 (lines 10–23)? What is the effect of this?

Grammar for reading

Impersonal writing is writing that does not have a person as its subject, for example, 'Meeting someone online is risky', rather than 'Don't meet anyone online, as it's risky'.

Purpose

6 The purpose of an advice text is to advise the reader to act in a particular way. What do you think is the main purpose of this magazine article? Provide evidence from the text to support your answer.

7 Paragraph 1 is really an information text.

   a) Why do advice texts often include information?

   b) What other text types does this article include, and what is their purpose?

 8 The three sections of the article are written and presented in different ways. Discuss these differences with a partner, and write them down. Why has the writer done this?

Reading for meaning

9 a) What is the purpose of the short section before the first proper paragraph of the article (lines 1–2)?

   b) How is it distinguished from the main article?

   c) What are the three dots (the ellipsis) doing at the end? Where else in the article are these dots used?

The word 'But' at the start of the second sentence is a connective. It is doing an important job:

> The connective 'but' signals to the reader that a different view is coming up in this sentence

> Upbeat, positive statement about pen pals

> ...pen pals can become friends for life. But the fact is, meeting someone via an internet club or through a magazine does have risks.

> Statement advising you that there may be risks involved

 10 a) Connectives are also useful in the middle of sentences. Discuss with a partner what job 'but' is doing in the following text from paragraph 2: 'Take meeting someone creepy online. It's awful, *but* you can log off quick sharp.'

   b) Can you spot a connective in paragraph 1 that signals that a reason is being given for a statement?

11 Four safety tips in the third section of the article are written as bullet points.

a) Why do you think the writer has done this?

b) What are the paragraphs above and below the bullet points doing?

Grammar for reading

Connectives are words that show how one sentence or clause is connected to another, for example, 'and', 'therefore', 'but'.

Exploring further: Writing to a pattern

12 The bullet-pointed safety tips have been written in a kind of pattern. With a partner, explore how the writing is similar in each bullet point, and discuss what effect this has.

Focus on: Informal language

The audience of *mizz* magazine is young teenage girls. So the writer uses **informal language** to 'speak to' this audience.

One common feature of informal language is the use of **contracted words**. You can usually spot a contracted word by the apostrophe. This tells you that one or more letters have been missed out.

For example: you're = you [a]re   I'd = I [woul]d

Another common feature of informal language is the use of **conversational** (or **colloquial**) **language**. This is language that is normally spoken rather than written, for example, 'mates', 'quick sharp', 'sussed'.

Watch out!

Sometimes an apostrophe may show *possession* instead, for example, 'Mike's book'.

13 Read through the 'Pen pal pointers' section and list the informal language that you find. Put it in a table with two columns like the one shown below.

Contractions	Conversational language
don't	first off
write'll	

Were there any words or phrases that you wanted to put in both columns?

Grammar for reading

Informal language doesn't follow the strict rules of grammar and style. It is used when a more relaxed and friendly tone is needed.

Exploring further: Conversational language

Slang and dialect are two common types of conversational language.

● **Slang** is at the most informal end of the spectrum. It is often used by members of a group (for example, schoolchildren) to show that they are different from others. Slang isn't often written down, and it changes a lot as fashions change.

● **Dialect** is a language variety that depends on where you live. For example, in the Midlands the dialect word for 'grumpy' is 'mardy'.

14 Can you identify any slang or dialect words in the article?

Key Writing

15 a) If you look carefully at the four bullet points in the article (lines 47–59), they are a mixture of formal and informal styles. The editor at *mizz* needs you to rewrite this section so that it matches the informal style of the rest of the article.

Remember:
● Use contractions and conversational language.
● Address the reader directly – use 'you' and commands.
● Present the heading in an eye-catching way.

b) Now imagine that you are addressing this section to the teenagers' parents. Write it again in a consistently formal style.

Unit 7 Assignment: Celebrity of the year

Assessment Focuses

- AF4 Construct paragraphs and use cohesion within and between paragraphs
- AF7 Select appropriate and effective vocabulary

> **You:** are taking part in a class debate.
>
> **Your task:** to write a short speech proposing your favourite celebrity as 'Celebrity of the Year'.

Stage 1

Choose your celebrity. He or she could be a pop star, a sportsperson, or an actor – anyone in the media, in fact.

Now think about why you admire him or her. Make a list of four or five qualities that make this person your top celebrity. For example:

Celebrity: **Kylie Minogue**
My celebrity of the year because of:

- her songs
- her looks
- her success
- her acting talent
- her fashion business.

Stage 2

You are going to write one paragraph on each quality.

First of all, decide which order you want the paragraphs to go in. Remember that you should have a powerful ending. You may want to save your best quality until last.

Stage 3

Now draft your four or five paragraphs. Remember to make your **main point** early in each paragraph and to use the other sentences in each paragraph to back up the main point. They can do this by giving a **reason**, by giving **evidence**, by referring to your own **experience** or by giving an **example** or **more detail** (see page 149).

For example:

Main point

Kylie is also very successful. For example, she has had 30 UK hits in a row.

Other sentence in paragraph gives the evidence for the main point

Read through your speech again and check how effective it is.

- Can you make any words more powerful or interesting?
- Are you going to give it a reasonable tone throughout, or a more persuasive tone? Whichever tone you choose, stick to it.
- Remember that this speech will be read aloud, so it must sound effective.

For example:

change 'very' to 'amazingly'

change 'hits' to 'smash hits'

> Kylie is also amazingly successful.
> Has anyone else had 30 smash
> hits in the UK – and all in a row?

use of question to grab
audience attention

use of pause (dash) for added effect

Finally, add a couple of sentences at the beginning to introduce your argument and add a couple more at the end to summarise your main points.

Challenge

- Practise speaking your argument aloud. Then put it to one side and speak in front of the class.

- You could use your notes from Stage 1 as prompts, or produce a Powerpoint version so you can refer to the notes as you speak, possibly using images of your celebrity as well.

- Speak confidently to win the class over to your point of view.

- Remember to end on a high point to really impress the audience.

① A visit to the doctor

Aims

❯ Read from an autobiography
❯ Learn how to skim and scan (R1, R2)
❯ Learn how to vary sentences
❯ Learn how to use simple and complex sentences (S1a, S1c)

In *Boy*, **Roald Dahl (1916–1990) recounts important events that happened to him. A visit to the doctor was one of them.**

A visit to the doctor

The doctor was bending over me. In his hand he held that long shiny steel instrument. He held it right in front of my face, and to this day I can still describe it perfectly. It was about the thickness and length of a pencil, and like most pencils it had a lot of sides to
5 it. Toward the end, the metal became much thinner, and at the very end of the thin bit of metal there was a tiny blade set at an angle. The blade wasn't more than a centimetre long, very small, very sharp and very shiny.

10 'Open your mouth,' the doctor said. Speaking Norwegian.
    I refused. I thought he was going to do something to my teeth, and everything anyone
15 has done to my teeth has been painful.

'It won't take two seconds,' the doctor said. He spoke gently, and I was seduced by his voice. Like an ass I opened my mouth.

20 The tiny blade flashed in the bright light and disappeared into my mouth. It went high up into the roof of my mouth, and the hand that held the blade gave four or five very quick little twists and the next moment, out of my mouth into the basin came tumbling a whole mass of flesh and blood.

I was too shocked and outraged to do anything but yelp. I was horrified by the huge red lumps that had fallen out of my mouth
25 into the white basin and my first thought was that the doctor had cut out the whole of the middle of my head.

'Those were your adenoids,' I heard the doctor saying.

I sat there gasping. The roof of my mouth seemed to be on fire. I grabbed my mother's arm and held on to it tight. I couldn't
30 believe that anyone would do this to me.

'Stay where you are,' the doctor said. 'You'll be all right in a minute.'

Blood was still coming out of my mouth and dripping into the basin the nurse was holding. 'Spit it all out,' she said, 'there's a
35 good boy.'

'You'll be able to breathe much better through your nose after this,' the doctor said.

The nurse wiped my lips and washed my face with a wet flannel. Then they lifted me out of the chair and stood me on my
40 feet. I felt a bit groggy.

'We'll get you home,' my mother said, taking my hand.

Down the stairs we went and on to the street. We started walking. I said *walking*. No trolley-car or taxi. We walked the full half-hour journey back to my grandparents' house, and when we
45 arrived at last, I can remember as clearly as anything my grandmother saying, 'Let him sit down in the chair and rest for a while. After all, he's had an operation.'

Someone placed a chair for me beside my grandmother's armchair, and I sat down. My grandmother reached over and
50 covered one of my hands in both of hers. 'That won't be the last time you'll go to a doctor in your life,' she said. 'And with a bit of luck, they won't do you too much harm.'

That was in 1924, and taking out a child's adenoids, and often the tonsils as well, without any anaesthetic was common practice
55 in those days. I wonder, though, what you would think if some doctor did that to you today.

•••••••••••••••••••••••••••••••••••

Key Reading

Autobiography

This text is an **autobiography**. It is a **recount**, in which the writer tells his life story. Its **purpose** is to recount or tell the reader about a series of events – in this case, Roald Dahl's early memories.

The main features of an autobiography are:

● It is mainly told in the **past tense**, for example, 'The tiny blade *flashed…*'

● It uses **time connectives** (words that tell the order of events), for example, '*That was* in 1924…'

● It is written in the **first person** (singular 'I' and plural 'we'), for example, '*I* was too shocked…'

● It includes **facts**, for example, 'Those were your adenoids…'

● It includes **opinions**, for example, 'I couldn't believe that anyone would do this to me.'

1 The first person plural (as well as singular) is used in the extract. Find an example and explain who it refers to.

2 What tense is the autobiography told in? Why?

3 When might the present tense be used in an autobiography?

•••••••••••••••••••••••••••••

Purpose

Although *Boy* is usually referred to as an autobiography, Roald Dahl did not see it like that. In the preface to the book he writes:

'An autobiography is a book a person writes about his own life and it is usually full of all sorts of boring details.

This is not an autobiography. I would never write a history of myself.'

4 He then goes on to say why he did write *Boy*. Can you guess why? The author's comment above gives a clue.

Reading for meaning

Skimming the text

When you read a text quickly for the first time, you can get a rough idea of what it is about and how it is told. This means you **skim** the text.

R1

5 a) What can you remember from your first reading? Quickly think of the main events in order.

b) Without reading the text, write down three questions asking where certain things occur in the text. Then ask a partner to answer them.

Scanning the text

If you want to find a piece of information in a text, you can **scan** it. This means skipping words to find what you are looking for. **Scanning** is a good way to get information quickly.

To find out what kind of operation Roald Dahl had, you could scan through the paragraphs until you find a key word such as 'adenoids'. For example, '"Those were your *adenoids*," I heard the doctor saying.'

R2

6 Scan the text for the following:

- the year that Roald Dahl had the operation
- what kind of transport the writer *could* have used to get home
- why the operation was performed
- who helped the doctor.

Exploring further: Time shift

In the final paragraph the text appears to shift in time so that the author is referring back to the events.

7 a) What time connectives at the beginning of the paragraph help to do this?

b) Is the voice in the text that of a boy or an adult here? Find words in the extract that give you clues.

• •

Focus on: Building tension

Varying sentences

When writing you may want to keep some information back until the end of a sentence or paragraph. Roald Dahl does this in paragraph 1:

> …out of my mouth into the basin came tumbling *a whole mass of flesh and blood.*

Dahl could have written:

> …*a whole mass of flesh and blood* came tumbling out of my mouth into the basin.

But by leaving the part that has the greatest impact until the end, the tension is kept up in the reader's mind.

S1c

8 a) Change this sentence around so that the tension is kept up: 'Maggots crawled from a purple gash when he turned the body over.'

b) Think of two more sentences of your own in which you:

● keep back the information with the greatest impact until the end

● can turn the sentence around.

Powerful description

Roald Dahl also uses another device to build up tension. If you study paragraph 1, you will see that he describes the doctor's scalpel in great detail. This is an important memory. He wants us to know all about it.

However, you can also think of this description as a way of building up tension. By taking time over the description, the author is delaying the awful action – and increasing the reader's interest.

R14

9 What does Dahl do in the final sentence of the paragraph to increase the tension further? Write down your answer.

Exploring further: Main and subordinate clauses

A **simple sentence** has one **main clause**. It usually has a subject, a verb and an object.

Verb

Subject —— He broke it. —— Object

However, some simple sentences only have a subject and a verb.

10 Which is the subject and which is the verb in this sentence?

'Maggots crawled.'

A **complex sentence** can have main clauses, subordinate clauses and phrases. Look at this sentence:

Main clause   Phrase   Subordinate clause

Maggots crawled from a purple gash when he turned the body over.

S1a

11 a) Identify the main clause and any subordinate clauses in the two sentences you wrote for question 8b.

b) Did you include any phrases? If so, label them.

167

Key Writing

Wr8

12 Recall an event in your life that was similar to Roald Dahl's operation. For example, it could be:

- a visit to the dentist
- having an inoculation
- a visit to the Accident and Emergency department.

Write a recount in two short paragraphs about this event.

S1c

- Use simple sentences and complex sentences to make your writing varied and more interesting.
- Keep some information back in key sentences to make an impact at the end of a paragraph.
- Try to use some time connectives so that the reader has a clear idea of the order of events.
- Also include a time shift, when you are referring back to the events.
- Write in the past tense.

Exploring further

13 Include a detailed description of a particular object or situation *before* or *after* the event. Roald Dahl describes the doctor's scalpel in detail before the operation. However, you could describe the situation *after* the incident, in that moment of shock before you fully realised what has happened.

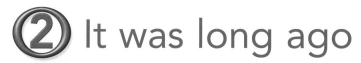 **It was long ago**

 Aims

❱ Read a poem

❱ Learn about rhythm and different kinds of rhyme (Wr8)

❱ Learn about the 'voice' of the poem

❱ Learn about repetition and use it to write your own poem (R14)

It Was Long Ago is a poem by Eleanor Farjeon (1881–1965) that has stood the test of time. As you read it, try to think why it is still read today.

It Was Long Ago

I'll tell you, shall I, something I remember?
Something that still means a great deal to me.
It was long ago.

A dusty road in summer I remember,
5   A mountain, and an old house, and a tree
That stood, you know,

Behind the house. An old woman I remember
In a red shawl with a grey cat on her knee
Humming under a tree.

10   She seemed the oldest thing I can remember,
But then perhaps I was not more than three.
It was long ago.

I dragged on the dusty road, and I remember
How the old woman looked over the fence at me
15 And seemed to know

How it felt to be three, and called out, I remember
'Do you like bilberries and cream for tea?'
I went under the tree

And while she hummed, and the cat purred, I remember
20 How she filled a saucer with berries and cream for me
So long ago,

Such berries and such cream as I remember
I never had seen before, and never see
To-day, you know.

25 And that is almost all I can remember,
The house, the mountain, the grey cat on her knee,
Her red shawl, and the tree,

And the taste of the berries, the feel of the sun I remember,
And the smell of everything that used to be
30 So long ago,

Till the heat on the road outside again I remember,
And how the long dusty road seemed to have for me
No end, you know.

This is the farthest thing I can remember.
35 It won't mean much to you. It does to me.
Then I grew up, you see.

Key Reading

Poetry

This text is a **poem**. Its **purpose** is to explore feelings and ideas.

A poem is made up of **images**, **rhythm** and **form**.

- The **images** are the pictures made by the words.
- The **rhythm** is like the beat in music.
- The **form** is the framework or pattern of the poem. Poems are written in lines not sentences.

Other important features of poems are:

- Some poems **rhyme**. For example, in *It Was Long Ago*, the words 'me', 'tree' and 'knee' rhyme.
- Some poems are **free verse**. They have lines of different lengths with different rhythms. (Some free verse contains rhyme.)

1 Read the first verse of *It Was Long Ago* again.

    a) What person is the poem written in?

    b) How old do you think the person is telling the poem? How can you tell?

2 **a)** What does the poet want to tell us about?

    b) Why do you think this is?

Purpose

It Was Long Ago explores feelings and ideas about childhood.

3 How does the last line of the poem make you feel? Write a sentence explaining your reaction.

4 The writer may have felt the same as you as she wrote. But in what way might she have felt differently when she had finished the poem? Write another sentence to explain.

Reading for meaning

Farjeon is looking back on a special memory and the poem is told like a story. The words 'I remember' are repeated throughout the poem. By repeating these words, Farjeon reminds the reader about the importance of her memories.

The same **rhyme pattern** is also used throughout. For example, the rhyme comes on the middle line of each three-line verse.

> I'll tell you, shall I, something I remember?
>
> Something that still means a great deal to <u>me</u>.
>
> It was long ago.
>
> A dusty road in summer I remember
>
> A mountain, and an old house, and a <u>tree</u>
>
> That stood, you know,

5 Quickly scan the other lines in the verses to find out how they rhyme. Where do the three main rhymes come in every verse?

R14

6 a) Find two other words or phrases that are repeated in these verses.

   b) What effect do they have?

7 How does the constant repetition emphasise the meaning of the poem? (Look back at your answer to question 2 for help.)

Exploring further: Rhyme

It Was Long Ago only has full rhyme at the end of its lines, but there are many other kinds of rhyme in poetry. Rhyme can occur at the start of a line (**beginning rhyme**) or in the middle (**internal rhyme**). They all have an effect on the poem. For example,

> Putting a *rhyme* in the middle of a *line*

The internal rhyme helps to make a rolling, thumping sound. This drives the poem along and is useful in comic poetry or nursery rhymes.

If we replaced the full rhymes in *It Was Long Ago* with some **half rhymes**, the poem would sound quite different. (In a half rhyme the vowel is not the same: send/wind, slept/slipped.)

8 a) Read verses 4 and 5 again. Then read the following, noting the change in the last line:

> She seemed the oldest thing I can remember,
>
> But then perhaps I was not more than three.
>
> It was long ago.
>
> I dragged on the dusty road, and I remember
>
> How the old woman looked over the fence at me
>
> It seemed she knew.

b) Thinking about what you have learned about rhyme, discuss why the poem only has **one** kind of rhyme (full rhyme) at the end of each line and not different kinds of rhyme.

Exploring further: The voice

When we read a text it seems as if the writer is speaking to us. But it is really the 'voice' of the text. Sometimes this voice can seem nearer to us than at other times, for example, when we are addressed directly, as in 'Dear reader…' or 'you'.

In *It Was Long Ago* the voice is close to us, particularly at certain moments. For example, in the first line ('I'll tell you, shall I, something I remember?') it almost seems as if the voice is asking us to reply.

9 The voice seems particularly close to us in two other places in the poem. Identify these and make a note of them.

• •

Focus on: Rhythm

All speech has **rhythm**. You can work out the rhythm of a speech by counting the syllables in certain words and listening to find out which syllables are stressed. For example, the word 'remember' has three syllables: re-mem-ber. When you say 'remember', the stress is put on the middle syllable. It is like a beat: re-*mem*-ber. The other two syllables in 'remember' are unstressed. In this way, the rhythms of speech are made up of **stressed** and **unstressed** syllables.

10 Which syllable is stressed in these words from the poem?

  ● something ● ago ● dusty ● perhaps ● bilberries

  (You could start by splitting the words into syllables.)

11 a) Choose a verse from the poem and write it out.

  b) Read each line and gently tap out the beat.

  c) Decide when the rhythm is the same and when it changes. Mark any changes in rhythm on your copy.

  d) Try the same thing with a different verse. Is the pattern of rhythm the same?

  e) Write a short explanation of whether *It Was Long Ago* has regular or irregular rhythm and why this suits the poem.

Key Writing

Grammar for reading

A **rhyming couplet** is two lines of poetry that have the same rhyme at the end. For example:

> In front of us, the great school *gate*,
> And all the thrill of being *late*.

 12 a) Think of a memory from your early childhood. It might be:

- linked to a special time, such as starting school or moving home
- the same memory you used for the Key Writing task on page 168.

b) Now choose from the following:

- Write a free verse poem about your memory.
  - Consider how you could include a rhyming couplet at regular intervals. (It does not have to be the same couplet, though it could be.)
  - Include repetition of a verse or line at regular intervals.
- Write a rhyming poem about your memory.
  - Decide whether the lines will be a mix of short and long, all short or all long. (The rhythm will be different depending on what you choose.)
  - Include repetition of key words or ideas in some way.

3 King Arthur: the truth (probably)

Aims

▶ Read an analysis text

▶ Learn how points are presented and questions asked

▶ Learn about connectives of cause, effect and contrast (W20)

▶ Look at how different tenses can be used in the same paragraph (S4)

▶ Take part in a group discussion about the reliability of evidence (S&L1)

The following case study of King Arthur is taken from a children's book that analyses stories from history against real source material.

King Arthur's Story

What's the story?

You mean you don't know? Well, there's this young lad. Called 'Wart' by his brother on account of being small and spotty, probably. One day a long time ago he sees a bloomin' great big rock. Thing is, it's got this magical-looking
5 sword sticking out of it, and if you pull it out you get to be Big Chief (well, King) of the Britons. But nobody, not even the biggest muscle-men, can remove it. But 'Wart' wanders up, and pulls it out, like it's a wobbly tooth. And so the legend is born. Arthur (ex-Wart), King of the Britons, leader of the Knights of the Round Table, has arrived.

10 ### Sounds a bit unlikely

Are you questioning the great Walt Disney? This is a scene from the animated film, *The Sword in the Stone*. It's a bit like all those other films about Arthur. You know the ones – *Excalibur* and, er, *Monty Python and the Holy Grail*. Plus, *King Arthur*. You must have heard of that one!

15   Well, usually Arthur and his knights sit around a Round Table (to show how equal they all are). Plus, there's Arthur's wife, the beautiful Guinivere – who has an 'affair' with Launcelot (one of Arthur's knights). And they all live happily at the castle of Camelot (well, Arthur wasn't that pleased, obviously).

Great for films, but is any of it true? Did Arthur even exist?

20 Let's look at the evidence:

Source 1: De Excidio Britanniae (6th century history book)
Who: Gildas (some British guy who wrote in Latin)

What: He mentions an important soldier, who might have been Arthur, at this great big battle in 5th century Roman Britain.

25   BUT...there's no mention of him being a 'king'

        AND...not definitely mentioned by name.

Source 2: **The Modena Cathedral Carving, Italy (around 1120)**
Who: Search me
30   What: Carving of a violent-looking bloke on horseback carrying a pointy thing (it's a lance, you idiot!). Funny writing reads *Artus de Bretania* (it's Latin, you fool!). This means 'Arthur of Britannia' (alright, clever clogs).

        BUT...*everyone* knew about Arthur – he was the Beckham of his day (except he didn't play football, and had been dead – if he existed – six hundred years so the carver may just have liked the story).

35   ## Is that it?

Are you joking? Everyone has something to say about Arthur!

Source 3: **'Historia Regum Britanniae' (another old history book– why can't these people write in English?)**
Who: Geoffrey of Monmouth (12th century)
40   What: He includes a romantic hero called Arthur.

        BUT...much of this 'history' was probably made-up.

        AND...Arthur may have become famous because King Henry II wanted to make people believe he was descended from him.

Source 4: **Arthur's grave at Glastonbury**
45   Who: Silly question
What: In 1191, in an old oak coffin, monks found the bodies of a huge man and a woman with golden hair. A cross made of lead inside read: 'Here lies the illustrious King Arthur buried in the Isle of Avalon.'

        BUT...It's probably a forgery! Historians reckon the monks did it 'cos they
50   needed money. And it worked. As a result, it brought the abbey immense fame and wealth.

So, what are you saying?

We can reveal exclusively that we really don't know. Ok, there *may* have been an important soldier with a name like 'Arthur'. And he *might* have been
55   around pointing sharp things at folk in the 5th or 6th centuries. But, most of the evidence is in the form of stories, poems or art. There are no bones or contemporary drawings of Arthur, as far as we know.

What about the Round Table?

Probably made-up by a Norman writer called Wace. Still, if you really want
60   one, there's a very good furniture shop I know...it's called 'Camelot Kitchens'...Only kidding.

Key Reading

Analysis texts

This text is an **analysis**. Its **purpose** is to study information or ideas closely, in this case to see if the information is reliable.

The main features of an analysis text are:

- It is told mainly in the **present tense**, although it sometimes switches to the **past tense** to give background information. For example:

  - when discussing the evidence the writer says, '*It's* probably a forgery' (present tense)

  - when saying how and when the evidence was discovered, the writer says, '...monks *found* the bodies of a huge man and a woman...' (past tense).

- Points are made clearly and backed up with **evidence**. For example, the evidence in the extract comes from historical sources such as facts, pictures and diagrams (like the Modena Cathedral Carving).

- It uses **connectives**, especially to do with contrast. For example, 'But...'

- It also uses **connectives** to do with **cause and effect**. For example, '...*As a result* [of the monks finding the grave of Arthur – the cause], it brought the abbey immense fame and wealth [the effect].'

- It uses **stylistic devices**, including **informal language** and **humour**, to engage the reader. For example, 'Funny writing reads *Artus de Bretania* (it's Latin, you fool!)'.

1 Who is the subject of the analysis on page 176–177?

2 a) How many sources of evidence are discussed?
   b) How old are each of the sources?

3 Which connective is repeated in each section to question the source?

A humorous version of King Arthur's story in Monty Python and the Holy Grail

4 Look at the last feature in the box on page 178: '…stylistic devices, including informal language and humour'. The writer of this analysis certainly uses a chatty, humorous style to break down the barrier between reader and writer. Can you find examples of the following techniques?

● Appearing to be in a conversation with the reader.

● Using brackets to add a comment or an extra thought (often humorous).

● Using modern words or phrases to replace more 'formal' or historical terms.

Purpose

5 What is the serious purpose behind the analysis? It is about an historical figure, but what is it trying to prove?

6 a) Which different *kinds* of evidence are looked at as sources?

b) Discuss why each source has been chosen. What does it tell the reader about Arthur's story?

7 The writer is not just concerned with this purpose; he also wants to analyse in an entertaining way. The layout of the text, as well as the use of humour, makes the text appealing. Identify the features of the layout that help to present the information clearly and make the text appealing.

8 The writer has used italics in the section headed, 'So what are you saying?' What effect does this have? What is being suggested about the statements containing the italicised words?

Reading for meaning

R8

9 a) The analysis uses questions for some headings. Who do you think is supposed to be asking the questions?

b) What attitude does the writer seem to have towards the questioner?

10 a) How reliable is the evidence (all four sources) that is discussed?

b) Which source (if any) do you find most convincing?

11 When the writer says, 'he was the Beckham of his day', what qualities is he suggesting Arthur had? Is this a good **analogy** or not?

Grammar for reading

When you use an **analogy** you draw parallels between, or compare, two quite different things, ideas or events in order to explain something. In the example above, the writer compares the qualities of King Arthur and David Beckham.

Changing tenses

Sometimes the writing changes from past to present tense in the same paragraph. For example:

- when referring to past events, it is written in the past tense
- when referring to what people think now, it is written in the present tense.

Launcelot with Arthur and Guinevere in King Arthur

12 Look at lines 43–51 about Arthur's grave.

- ● Underline all the past tense verbs.
- ● Circle all the present tense verbs.

13 Now, imagine you are looking at a photograph of yourself aged five. You are wearing your favourite clothes from that time.

a) First write some sentences about yourself at five years old, in the *past tense*.

b) Then write some sentences commenting on the clothes in the picture. Do this in the *present tense*. Remember, you are commenting *now*.

• •

Focus on: Using connectives of cause, effect and contrast

You can use connectives to link **cause** (reason) and **effect** (what happens). For example:

cause   connective

We wanted to find out if Arthur was a real person, **so** we studied the carving.

effect

You could also write the sentence this way:

We studied the carving **because** we wanted to find out if Arthur was a real person.

14 How has the sentence been altered? Can you say *why* it had to be changed?

15 Choose the right connective to turn these two sentences into one longer sentence. Then write out the new sentence.

The monks wanted to make Glastonbury famous. They discovered Arthur's grave.

The other main type of connective used in the extract is one that shows two contrasting points of view. Usually, this appears as 'BUT...' in the text.

Here is another source of evidence and a sentence suggesting that this evidence is unreliable:

> Thomas Malory wrote a whole book about Arthur in 1470. It wasn't based on historical facts.

16 Write these two sentences as one sentence, using a different connective from 'but' to link the two, to *qualify* the first statement. This means that the connective will not make the evidence sound incorrect, but instead will modify or qualify what is being suggested.

Key Speaking and Listening

17 In groups, discuss the evidence about King Arthur.

    a) Decide whether there really *was* a King Arthur. In your discussion, use connectives such as 'but', 'however', 'so' and 'because'. You can then discuss *why* the legend of Arthur has survived.

    b) After the discussion, consider how well you:
- explained your views
- listened to the views of others in the group
- used helpful connectives
- referred to clues or evidence from the sources.

Exploring further

A key skill in effective group discussions is to report back your findings. This may mean reporting a decision or discussion to another person or you may have to report back to a larger group.

18 a) Make a 'mental note' of the key things your group discussed. Write them down in simple notes, for example, 'Group agreed Arthur not real'.

    b) Now, with your notes to hand, report back your group's findings to a member of another group. Stick to the main points you discussed. Then listen to *their* findings.

④ Unit 8 Assignment: The historian's analysis

Assessment Focus

▶ AF3 Organise and present whole texts effectively, sequencing and structuring information, ideas and events

---

You: are an historian. You study evidence about the past.

Your task: to write an analysis and an assessment of the evidence. When you assess the evidence you must decide how useful it is to an historian.

. . . .

Stage 1

You have a list of questions to ask about the evidence. Complete the list by writing further questions. Under the heading 'Assessment of the evidence', what is the most important question you must ask?

Information

a) What kind of evidence is it? (For example, an object, a picture or written evidence?)

b) Where does it come from? (For example, a book or a newspaper?)

c) When was it made or written?

d)

e)

Questions about written evidence

f) Are there any interviews? If yes, who with?

g)

h)

Assessment of the evidence

i) What useful things does it tell us about the past?

j)

k)

183

Source A

There is another class who may be termed river-finders…they are commonly known by the name of 'mud-larks' from being compelled, in order to obtain the articles they seek, to wade sometimes up to their middle through the mud left on the (river) shore…

The mud-larks collect whatever they happen to find, such as coals, bits of old iron, rope, bones, and copper nails that drop from ships while lying or repairing along shore… The coals…they sell to the poor people of the neighbourhood.

From *London Labour and the London Poor* by Henry Mayhew, 1861.

Source B

'It is very cold in winter' he said, 'to stand in the mud without shoes'… He had been three years mud-larking, and supposed he should remain a mud-lark all his life. What else could he be?

Comments from a boy aged nine in London Labour and the London Poor by Henry Mayhew, 1861.

Stage 2

Check the evidence against the questions and write your notes. For example:

> Information about Source B
> a) Written evidence
> b) A book
> c) 1861

Stage 3

Use your notes to write three paragraphs that analyse the evidence in Sources A and B.

Remember:

● Write mainly in the present tense.

● Use other tenses as you need to.

● Give your paragraphs subheadings. Refer to the notes to decide what these might be.

● Use a range of connectives. For example, use connectives of contrast and qualification when you are assessing the evidence, such as:

- 'However'   - 'On the other hand'
- 'Having said that'   - 'But'
- 'Yet'   - 'Although'

Challenge

Carry out some research of your own into mud-larks.

● Use the library and the Internet. If you can, refer to Henry Mayhew's book *London Labour and the London Poor: Volume II Scavengers and Cleaners* and other sources. (Remember to use the Internet under your teacher's guidance.)

● Select information and make notes.

● Write a full account of the mud-lark's life and refer to evidence, including illustrations.

● In your analysis discuss the usefulness of the evidence you have found. (For example, think about the date of the source material as well as what it tells you.)

Unit 9 Sporting challenge

 Ellen MacArthur's inspiration

Aims

▷ Read a profile about a famous yachtswoman
▷ Learn how to search for key information (R1)
▷ Learn how to make clear notes from information you have read (R4)
▷ Look at other ways of making notes for different purposes
▷ Practise recording information sources

This text is from a BBC news website article about the young yachtswoman, Ellen MacArthur. It describes how she became a sailor.

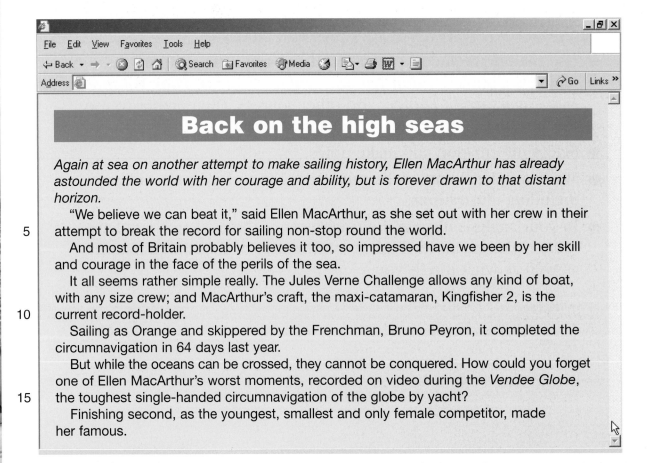

Back on the high seas

Again at sea on another attempt to make sailing history, Ellen MacArthur has already astounded the world with her courage and ability, but is forever drawn to that distant horizon.

"We believe we can beat it," said Ellen MacArthur, as she set out with her crew in their attempt to break the record for sailing non-stop round the world.

And most of Britain probably believes it too, so impressed have we been by her skill and courage in the face of the perils of the sea.

It all seems rather simple really. The Jules Verne Challenge allows any kind of boat, with any size crew; and MacArthur's craft, the maxi-catamaran, Kingfisher 2, is the current record-holder.

Sailing as Orange and skippered by the Frenchman, Bruno Peyron, it completed the circumnavigation in 64 days last year.

But while the oceans can be crossed, they cannot be conquered. How could you forget one of Ellen MacArthur's worst moments, recorded on video during the *Vendee Globe*, the toughest single-handed circumnavigation of the globe by yacht?

Finishing second, as the youngest, smallest and only female competitor, made her famous.

But no one would have exchanged places
with her as she scaled a 90-foot mast to
20 battle with torn sails during a violent squall
near the Equator – "like trying to hang on to
a telegraph pole in an earthquake".

"It's just too much," she sobbed to the
camera.

25 But MacArthur says the sailor's self-
preservation system "makes you forget just
how bad things were – otherwise, you
would be in too much shock. And it's that
which allows you to go back out there and
30 do it again".

Her biggest fear is "probably failure".
When she was 10, she came last in all the
races at a sailing school, where most of the
youngsters had better boats and equipment.

35 "On the journey home I decided that I
would never let this happen again," she
recalled. "I wasn't going to be last, no matter
what it took."

Tomboy

40 Ellen MacArthur comes from Whatstandwell
in landlocked Derbyshire, but as soon as
she could read, she savoured the pleasures of Arthur Ransome's *Swallows and
Amazons*.

By the time she was eight, and taking regular trips in her Auntie Thea's sloop off the
45 Essex coast, she was hooked on sailing.

She saved her school dinner money for three years to help buy her own boat, an eight-
foot dinghy named Threep'ny Bit. At home, she slept in a sleeping bag in the garage, to
make room for all her charts in her bedroom.

"I didn't have many friends at school", she says. "I always spent more time with the
50 boys, because they didn't do girls' things."

At 18, she sailed single-handed round Britain and won the Young Sailor of the Year award.

But it wasn't until she took part in a solo race across the Atlantic in 1997 that little Ellen,
5 ft 2 in with eyes of blue, attracted major sponsorship, from Kingfisher, the stores group.

Inspiration

55 It was Ellen's grandmother, Irene Lewis, who made it possible to enter her first big race.

She left Ellen £5,000 in her will, enabling her to pay the entrance fee for the
Vendee Globe.

But her nan also provided inspiration. She was 82 when she graduated from Derby
University despite suffering from lung cancer. She died three months later.

60 This example of courage helped Ellen MacArthur to realise her dream and to tell her
story in an autobiography, *Taking on the World*.

She became an international heroine, and particularly in France where her
achievements, complemented by her fluent French, led one journalist to call her "the
greatest Englishwoman since Jane Austen".

65 Now 26, she lives in a one-bedroom flat at Cowes on the Isle of Wight. But her
emotional home is the sea, a romance which the man in her life accepts with pragmatism.

Key Reading

Recount texts

This text is a **recount**. Its **purpose** is to recount or tell the reader about a series of events.

The main features of a recount text are:

- It is mainly told in the **past tense**, for example, 'She *sailed* single-handed round Britain.'

- It describes events in **time order** (chronological order), for example, we are told that Ellen was sailing regularly 'by the time she was eight'.

- It uses **time connectives** (words that tell you the order of events) and refers to specific dates, names of people and places, and time spans or shifts, for example, 'by the time', 'until'.

1 The text is mainly about Ellen MacArthur, but who else is mentioned – and what connection do they have with Ellen?

S13b 2 Look through the text from the heading 'Tomboy' onwards, and find examples of each of the three main features of recount texts.

3 **a)** The first half of this text (up to the heading 'Tomboy') mostly uses the present tense. Why is this?

   b) Why do you think it changes to (mostly) past tense use in the second half?

4 The chronological structure of the text is interesting in other ways. The grid below shows how the time structure of the text works. Copy and complete it:

Text	Time (now, the past, specific time?)
lines 4–10	Ellen speaking **now** (in the present). Details about the race happening **now**.
lines 11–12	Writer tells us about Bruno Peyron, another sailor and what he did '**last year**' (in the past).
lines	
lines	
lines	
lines	

Purpose

5 What do you think the main purpose of this text is? Support your opinion with *direct reference* to the text. For example, if you feel it is to show people that hardship leads to success, find evidence for this.

Reading for meaning

The text is divided into three sections, two of which have a **subheading**. Remember, a subheading goes underneath a main title or heading. It is usually smaller in size than the main title.

6 The two subheadings in the Ellen MacArthur text are 'Tomboy' and 'Inspiration'. Who do they each refer to?

7 What would be a suitable subheading for the first part of the text? Remember, a subheading can either summarise the whole or the overall focus of a section, or signal a particular point of interest or detail. (Consider whether the purpose of the other two subheadings is to signal one interesting detail or to sum up the main focus.)

Exploring further: Drawing conclusions

One of the features of this text is that we find out very little about the writer's personal feelings. But we can still draw conclusions from what he includes and doesn't include. For example, he mentions Ellen's grandmother *but* doesn't mention her parents.

8 What might we conclude (rightly or wrongly) from this?

9 Write an account of about 175 words in which you describe the *impression* do we get of Ellen from the article, supporting what you say with reasons. For example, is she lazy? Does she give up easily? You could begin:

'I think the impression given of Ellen is that she is...'

· ·

Focus on: Finding information and making clear notes

Imagine that you have to write an article about Ellen MacArthur. To do this, you need to find the **right information**.

R1 **10** Which of these pieces of information would be useful to your article?

> Ellen's nan was 82 when she graduated from Derby University.

OR

> Ellen saved her school dinner money for three years to help buy her own boat.

R4 **11** Now look through the article and make notes in the form of a list about the things Ellen did that were inspiring. Make sure that you only include the key points. For example, lines 44 and 45 become:

> Ellen, 8, in Aunt's boat, Essex coast

Notice how the points on the list are not the same as the original text in the article. As you complete the list, remember to:

● **cut out** any words or phrases that **you don't need**

● **shorten** or make information **more simple**.

Exploring further: Different ways of note-making

When you are planning your writing, it is sometimes helpful to make notes using a different format, such as a spider diagram.

12 This spider diagram is one that the author might have used when he was planning his article. What parts of the plan are missing? Copy and complete the plan.

What Ellen is doing now   Gran's influence   First achievements

Ellen article

Key Writing

13 Find a source of information about a famous sportsman or sportswoman. Use a reference book or a specialist magazine, or look on the Internet. Then make notes using a grid like the one below.

Notes/headings	Information	Source
Early life		
First significant achievement/s		
First public success		
Difficulties/complications		
Current situation		

Remember:

● Make a note of the *source* of the information (where it came from). For example:

 – a web address (www.bbc.co.uk/sportacademy)

 – a book title, editor/author and publisher (*The Faber Book of Soccer*, ed. Iain Hamilton)

 – another source, such as a magazine (*Four Four Two* magazine)

● Make the information notes brief and clear.

14 Use your notes to draft a 'profile' of your sports personality, using the Ellen MacArthur text as a model. Think carefully about how you will order your sections to tell the reader about your sportsperson's life.

 ● Remember that recounts mostly use the past tense, but you may wish to start with the present tense to describe what your personality is doing *now*.

 ● Try slotting in comments by your personality or by people who know him or her.

② Bend it like Beckham

Aims

) Read an extract from a novel

) Develop the skill of looking for key words (R1)

) Learn more about speech punctuation (S7)

) Write your own text using direct speech

The following text is from a book by Narinder Dhami about Jess Bhamra, a British Indian girl who plays football. Her team is in a big final, but it is also her sister's wedding day. Jess's father has just overheard her speaking with her friend Tony at the wedding about the match. Tony urges Jess's father to let her go – but Jess feels guilty.

Bend it like Beckham

'Stop it, Tony,' I broke in. 'Dad, it doesn't matter. This is much more important. I don't want to spoil the day for you and Mum.'

Dad looked at me steadily. 'Pinky is so happy today,' he said abruptly. 'And you, you look like you're at your father's funeral.'

I hung my head. 'I'm sorry, Dad.'

'If this is the only way I'm going to see you smiling on your sister's wedding day, then go.' I jerked my head up, hardly able to believe my ears. 'But when you come back, I want to see you happy on the video.'

This time the big smile on my face was for real. I threw my arms round Dad and hugged him tightly.

'Play well, and make us proud,' he whispered in my ear.

The game would have already started by the time we got there, but I wouldn't have missed much. Tony took me home to grab my kit, and then drove as fast as the speed limit would let him towards the ground. Meanwhile, I was in the back seat, unwrapping my sari to save time. I wriggled into my kit and kicked off Mrs Paxton's shoes with the diamante bows. As I laced up my boots, Tony spun into the car park and ground to a screeching halt.

5

10

15

20

25

I leapt out of the car, and ran towards the pitch.

My adrenaline was rocketing as I pushed my way through the crowd and vaulted over the barrier, rushing over to Joe who was standing shouting on the touchline. His face broke into a huge smile when he saw me, but he didn't stop to ask any questions.

'Start warming up, Bhamra,' he said, giving my shoulder a squeeze. 'We're one-nil down.'

One-nil down. That was a bit of a shock. Still, there was plenty of time for us to come back. We were only about twenty minutes into the first half.

I did my stretches, then jogged impatiently on the touchline, waiting for my chance to get on to the pitch. It came when Mel fouled one of the other team, and they got a free kick. I dashed on to the field as a sub, getting patted on the back and cheered by the other Harriers as I passed. Jules had only just noticed me, and her mouth dropped open in amazement.

'I'm so glad you came!' she yelled, giving me a huge hug. Relief surged through me. It was going to be OK.

Together, we lined up alongside the others to make a defensive wall, as one of the QPR players placed the ball for their free kick. They were only just outside the penalty area, and this was their chance to grab another goal. I could feel the blood rushing in my ears as I watched the player run up to take it. Being two down would be no joke. But the ball sailed over the top of the wall, and Charlie caught it safely.

Now that Jules and I were back in business as friends *and* team-mates, we played better than ever. Our passes were fast and sharp and accurate, and we moved smoothly down the pitch, almost reading each other's minds as the ball flew between us. We were ripping the heart out of the QPR defence. It was only a matter of time before we scored.

I watched as Mel passed the ball to Jules while we ran from the centre into the QPR half. I knew what Jules was going to do – and she did it. She let the ball roll through her legs to me, completely fooling the QPR defence. I picked it up quickly behind her, allowing Jules to run forward nearer to the goal, then I threaded a neat pass towards her. Jules was on to it in a flash, and a second later the ball was sitting in the corner of the net.

Jules screamed 'YES!' and ran round the pitch with her top over her head, showing off her sports bra. I couldn't stop laughing. Joe was going mad on the touchline, while the rest of us jumped on top of Jules, hugging her to death.

Key Reading

Narrative texts

This text is a **narrative**. Its **purpose** is to tell a story.

The main features of a narrative text are:

● It has a structure that includes an opening (**introduction**), a problem (**complication**), a dramatic moment when everything comes to a head (**crisis**) and an ending (**resolution**) when things are sorted out. For example, *Bend it like Beckham* has the following structure:

Introduction: We find out about Jess and her love of football.

Complication: Jess joins a football team secretly but her parents find out and are not happy.

Crisis: Jess is set to play in a final but it is her sister's wedding.

Resolution: Jess's dad finally allows her to play in the match.

● It has **characters** who the story is about. You often hear their words and thoughts in direct speech, shown by speech marks. For example, 'Jules screamed "YES!"'.

● There is also a **narrator** who tells the story. In this case the narrator is the main character, Jess.

● It includes **powerful description**. For example, 'We were *ripping the heart out* of the QPR defence.'

1 The extract is divided into several separate scenes which would work well in a film version.

　● What are the separate scenes that we see (one quite briefly)?

　● Who is narrating these scenes?

2 There are several examples of direct speech in the extract. Find each one, and then decide:

　● Who is speaking?

　● How do we know?

3 The writer uses at least two expressions that create strong images in the reader's mind. One relates to Jess's feelings as her team defend the free-kick. The other relates to how her team are attacking QPR's defence.

   a) Can you find the two descriptions?

   b) What do they seem to suggest about Jess's feelings and emotions?

Purpose

4 The purpose of *Bend it like Beckham* is to tell a story and to **entertain** the reader. How does the writer achieve these? Consider:

   - the characters and their relationships
   - the way the events are presented – the wedding, the drive to the match, the match itself.

5 The writer reveals certain things about the characters' feelings in this extract. How does she do this? Read the text again, from Jess's arrival at the match, and find evidence for the feelings. Then add it to the table below.

Character	Feelings	Evidence from the text
Jess	Excited but concerned about the game.	
Joe	Pleased to see Jess.	
Jules	Shocked but pleased to see Jess.	

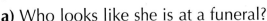

Reading for meaning

When we are exploring how a text works, one way of finding basic 'surface' information is to look at the **key words** from questions we need to know the answers to. For example:

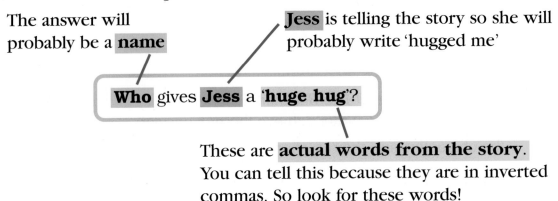

The answer will probably be a **name**

Jess is telling the story so she will probably write 'hugged me'

Who gives **Jess** a 'huge hug'?

These are **actual words from the story**. You can tell this because they are in inverted commas. So look for these words!

Sometimes the words in the question *are not* in the story but **similar** or **connected** words are. For example:

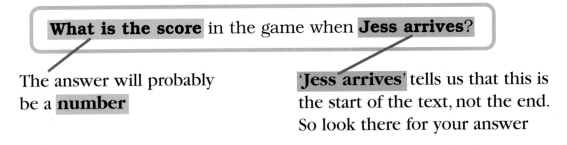

What is the score in the game when **Jess arrives**?

The answer will probably be a **number**

'Jess arrives' tells us that this is the start of the text, not the end. So look there for your answer

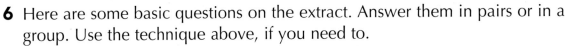

R1

6 Here are some basic questions on the extract. Answer them in pairs or in a group. Use the technique above, if you need to.

  a) Who looks like she is at a funeral?

  b) Where and how did Jess manage to get changed into her kit before the game?

  c) Who gives Jess a 'huge hug'?

  d) How did Jules fool the QPR defence?

Apart from the last question above, most of the answers can be found in a fairly straightforward way. However, where characters' feelings are **implied** or suggested rather than told to us directly, we cannot always use key words to find the information.

How would you answer this question?: 'How do you think Jess's father feels?'

● First, check the key words: 'How' + 'Jess's father' + 'feels'.

● Then, scan the text to see where he appears: at the start, page 192, paragraph 2.

● Then note down what he says and does: He overhears Tony and Jess's conversation. He lets Jess go to the match. He wishes her luck. He doesn't want the family day ruined.

7 Draw conclusions from what you have found out. Answer the question in your own words.

Exploring further: The function of paragraphs

In a story, the writer can tell us lots of information in one paragraph, but often there is one overall **paragraph focus**. For example, in the paragraph starting 'Together, we lined up…' the main focus is *defending the free-kick*.

8 Decide on a paragraph focus for each of the last three paragraphs on page 193.

- -

Focus on: How to punctuate speech in longer sentences

Speech is normally punctuated like this:

Insert **space** (indent text) left from margin

A **full-stop** ends the sentence in the normal way

'I'm so glad you came!' she yelled.

Opening speech marks are placed in front of the first word that is spoken

Punctuation to do with what is being said goes **in front of the final speech marks.** Here it is an **exclamation mark** because the speaker is yelling. Normally, a **comma** is used

Closing speech marks are placed after the last word that is spoken

Remember, *every time* the speaker **changes** in a conversation you must start **a new line**.

Now, look at this longer piece of speech from the extract:

> 'Start warming up, Bhamra,' he said, giving my shoulder a squeeze. 'We're one-nil down.'

Note that the first sentence follows the same rules. However:

- There is an **extra** bit of speech. This is still said by Joe, so it is not a new paragraph.
- Because we know it is Joe speaking ('he said') the writer does not need to say 'Joe said' or 'he said' again.
- As it is the end of what Joe is saying, there has to be a full-stop before the last speech mark.

S7

9 Make notes on the following piece of dialogue from the extract. You will need to label the points made in all three examples above.

> 'Stop it, Tony,' I broke in. 'Dad, it doesn't matter. This is much more important. I don't want to spoil the day for you and Mum.'
>
> Dad looked at me steadily. 'Pinky is so happy today,' he said abruptly. 'And you, you look like you're at your father's funeral.'
>
> I hung my head. 'I'm sorry, Dad.'

• •

Key Writing

Wr5

10 Continue the story from the end of the extract. Imagine that Jess runs up to congratulate Jules after she finishes her goal celebration as the whistle blows for the end of the first half. Include:

- three or four pieces of dialogue
- some information about the girls and their feelings. This can be direct or implied information.

For example, you could start like this:

I ran up to Jules as she came back from the crowd.
'That was a great goal. I knew we could do it,' I shouted.

Once you have finished, go through your paragraphs and see if there are any opportunities to add extra information or details.

③ Top bike techniques

Aims

◗ Read a text about how to learn mountain biking skills

◗ Look at how instructions are written (S13d)

◗ Understand and use imperative verbs

◗ Explore time connectives (W20)

◗ Compose your own instruction text (Wr13)

This text is taken from a book on how to learn mountain biking skills.

Advanced mountain biking techniques

The more you ride, the more you can improve your basic techniques so that your ride is faster, more comfortable and more controlled.

5   For advanced moves, such as the bunny-hop, develop the ability to transfer your weight on your bike, skillfully and smoothly. Move your weight backwards to reduce the weight on the front wheel. Move your weight

10   forwards to lighten the weight on the rear wheel. To alter the amount the bike leans when you take a corner, transfer your weight from side to side.

Soon you will be able to make the bike do anything you want!

Cornering at speed

15   To corner at speed, keep the leg and pedal on the outside of the turn in a downwards position. Keep the leg on the inside of the turn away from the pedal, ready to put it down in case you lean over too far.

Professional riders "drift", or skid, through corners, steering in

20   the opposite direction to control a skid with both wheels sliding sideways, and applying the brakes. It's dramatic – but best left to the professionals!

Jumps ▐

25 Hitting a small lump in the trail can lift the bike in the air. Jumping is great, but because the bike is in the air, you're in more danger of hurting yourself. Start with small jumps; only progress to larger ones when you are confident. When you land, bend your arms and legs to reduce the impact of the bike as it lands.

30 ### *The bunny-hop* ▐

The bunny-hop allows you to lift both wheels clear of the ground at the same time. To look at it, you'd think it was impossible, but it's not! It is a useful move, 35 especially if you come across a log or a pothole on the trail.

Begin with a single-wheel bunny-hop. Ride 40 at a walking pace; crouch down and pull back on the handlebars as you push down on the pedals.

45 As you do this, the front wheel will lift off the ground. Shift your weight forwards, pushing down on the handlebars. 50 This will lift the back wheel off the ground as the front wheel clears the obstacle. As you land, start to pedal.

55 For the double-wheel bunny-hop, stay out of the saddle and crouch down. Pull on the handlebars and jump or spring the bike clear of the 60 obstacle. Not easy, but practice makes perfect.

Key Reading

Instruction texts

This is an **instruction** text. Its **purpose** is to tell someone clearly how to do something.

The main features of an instruction text are:

● It usually has a **clear design**, with a **step-by-step** approach often supported by **pictures** or **diagrams**, for example, photos that show the move.

● It has a **plain and simple** style, often using **connectives** of **time** or **sequence**, for example, 'When you land, bend your arms and legs to reduce the impact.' You need to be able to understand the instructions and follow them easily.

● It uses **imperative** verbs. These are verbs that **tell** (or **command**) you to do something, for example, 'Pull on the handlebars.'

S13d

1 a) What is this text instructing the reader about?

b) Is this a text for experienced bikers or bikers interested in learning new skills?

2 What is the key time/sequence word that means 'at the same time' that is used three times in the last paragraph but one of the extract?

3 Find three technical terms (words or phrases) to do with biking in the extract.

Grammar for reading

In instruction texts such as this, most **imperative verbs** are to do with single, physical actions, for example: 'Pull on the handlebars'. Sometimes, however, texts use more general verbs to introduce ideas or sum up a sequence of instructions. For example:

General verb used
to introduce the
'whole' idea

How to **impress** girls!

First, **clean** your teeth!

Give her flowers!

Specific verbs
for instructions

4 Which of these phrases from the text are specific instructions and which are more general?:

- 'develop the ability'
- 'move your weight forwards'
- 'begin with a single-wheel bunny hop'
- 'progress to larger ones when you are confident.'

• •

Purpose

The purpose of the text is to make the instructions **clear** and **easy to follow**. As you have seen, this is aided by the use of **imperatives**.

In *Advanced mountain biking techniques*, the writer uses imperatives to **tell** the beginner exactly what he or she must do. For example:

> Move your weight backwards to reduce the weight on the front wheel.

Putting 'move' at the front of the sentence makes it very powerful. Not all imperatives appear at the start of sentences, but many do. This instruction is a **command**.

5 How would the tone and effect of the instruction change if it said: '*You might like to* move your weight…', or '*It could be good if* you moved your weight…'?

6 Look at the following instruction.

> Look in your mirror before you reverse the car.

Add each of the following beginnings to the instruction above and then decide how they each change the tone and effect of the sentence. (You may have to add '–ing' to the imperative verb to make it work.)

- Why don't you…
- It might be a good idea to…
- How about…
- You could…

Exploring further: Adapting verbs to fit purpose

7 Here is a short dialogue between a waiter and a customer. Rewrite it so the waiter is more polite. You might have to change more than just the verb.

Waiter:	Sit down at this table.
Man:	Err, thanks. Right – here we are darling.
Waiter:	Give me your coat.
Woman:	Here. Thank you.
Waiter:	Have this menu. ~~Order some drinks~~. Could I take your order?
Man:	Now, hang on – we've never been spoken to like this before.
Waiter:	Find another restaurant.

Reading for meaning

8 The fact that *Advanced mountain biking techniques* is an instruction text is supported by the way it is separated into chunks. Each chunk or section has a different function. Complete this matching task, fitting each section to its purpose.

Section	Purpose
Opening section	Deals with a specific skill
Cornering at speed	Gives general advice
Jumps	Deals with a specific skill
The bunny-hop	Deals with a general skill

9 In the first section, the writer uses a number of *adverbs* or phrases that act like adverbs, to describe how or where to move. These are vital in understanding how the writer has constructed the instructions. List all the adverbs in the first section.

Grammar for reading

An **adverb** describes *how* you do something. It goes with a **verb**. We often expect adverbs to end in *-ly* (for example, 'quietly', 'curiously') but there are many adverbs that don't, such as 'backwards'.

10 This extract comes from a book for young people aged 10–13, designed to teach them biking techniques. The designers could have chosen a number of other ways to present these instructions.

a) Discuss any improvements you would make to the text and layout. Consider:

- language and vocabulary
- layout – headings, subheadings, where the text is placed
- use of images, and where they are placed
- any other suggestions.

b) Feed back your answers to another pair. Did you have similar ideas?

• •

Focus on: Instructions that are easy to follow

Clear instructions need imperative verbs, such as 'place', 'put' or 'keep'. However, instructions can also contain reasons *why* something should be done. The reason or effects described can be good or bad.

Instruction	
Keep your eyes on the road... ⟶	

Note the use of the word 'or' to show what *might* happen.

Here is another example taken from the text:

Instruction

When you land, **bend your arms and legs** to **reduce the impact** of the bike as it lands.

Reason (good)

11 Use the situations below to write down five warnings which use 'or' to show the effect or outcome of any action. For example, 'Keep your eye on the pancake when you flip it in the air *or it might land on your head*'.

● Checking your parachute before you jump.

● Asking your dad for pocket money.

● Listening to all the tracks on a CD before you buy it.

● Telling someone a secret.

● Painting your room a new colour.

● ●

Key Writing

Wr13

12 You and your friends have been given the task of organising a mini-tournament for football or basketball for four local primary schools. The teams need to arrive at your school at 9 am on Saturday morning.

You need to send out a set of instructions to all the parents about:

● what their children need to wear

● what they need to bring

● when to arrive

● when the final will be played

● when the parents need to pick their children up.

S&L10

a) Discuss the instructions you need to send, then make a list of those that you all agree on. Remember to do the following:

● Start (where you can) with an imperative verb. For example, 'Arrive at…'.

● Use sequence words if needed, such as 'Afterwards…'.

● Include any other information. For example, 'The winners will each get a medal…'.

b) Design a poster for the mini-tournament. Use your instructions and make them briefer. Make sure all your instructions are clear and suitable for your audience. Include an image that will make people want to come along.

④ Unit 9 Assignment: Sports reporter

 Assessment Focuses

▷ AF4 Construct paragraphs and use cohesion within and between paragraphs

▷ AF5 Vary sentences for clarity, purpose and effect

> **You:** are the reporter for a football magazine.
>
> **Your task:** to write a profile of Thierry Henry for the magazine.

Stage 1

You have already interviewed Thierry Henry and your notes are shown below. Unfortunately, they are not well organised.

Captained French under-18 team.
Born 17 August 1977 in Paris, France.
Signed for First Division Monaco under manager Arsene Wenger aged 13.
Scored most goals for France in 1998 World Cup.
Studied at prestigious L'Institut National de Football in Clairfontaine.
Signed for Arsenal in Aug 1999. Renewed working relationship with Arsene Wenger.
Named PFA Players' Player of the Year in 2003 and 2004.
Given red card in World Cup match against Uruguay in 2002.
Married to model Nicole Merry. Met while filming TV ad for Renault.
Brought up in a poor suburb of Paris. Had a lot of support from family.
Signed for Juventus in Jan 1999.
Played first professional game for Monaco aged 17.
First game for France against South Africa in 1997.
Helped Arsenal to unbeaten run in 2003/2004 Premiership season.

Stage 2

Organise the notes. Choose suitable sub-headings for each section of the profile, for example, 'Early life'.

Stage 3

Turn the notes into a **profile**. Remember to write in full sentences and to use the **past tense** for the main part of the profile, but use the **present tense** for the opening sentences and closing comments which will describe where Thierry comes from and his current situation. You should also use **subheadings** for each section, include **time connectives** where appropriate and try to include some **direct speech**, perhaps about Thierry's feelings.

For example, you could turn the following notes into the sentences below:

Early life

Thierry Henry
Born 1977
Lots of support from family

➡

Early life

Thierry Henry was born in 1977 and first played professionally aged 17.
    'My family were always supportive,' he told me.

Time connective

Challenge

Although many recount texts focus on facts, there will be occasions when powerful individual moments are described in ways very similar to narrative texts. An example of this is lines 18–24 on page 187.

Expand one of the points from your profile by adding more descriptive detail to it. You may need to use your imagination and remember to use powerful language. For example:

'Who can forget Thierry's classic performances at the 1998 World Cup? It was his contribution there that played a major part in the French team's eventual victory...'

...ed by Collins
...mprint of HarperCollins*Publishers*
.7–85 Fulham Palace Road
Hammersmith
London
W6 8JB

Browse the complete Collins catalogue at
www.collinseducation.com

© HarperCollins*Publishers* Limited 2004

10 9 8 7 6 5 4 3 2 1

ISBN 0 00 719434 X

Mike Gould, Mary Green, John Mannion and Kim Richardson assert their moral
rights to be identified as the authors of this work

British Library Cataloguing in Publication Data
A Catalogue record for this publication is available from the British Library

Acknowledgements

The following permissions to reproduce material are gratefully
acknowledged:

Text: *The Shortest Horror Story Ever Written* from MORE HOROWITZ
HORROR by Anthony Horowitz first published in the UK by Orchard
Books in 2000, a division of The Watts Publishing Group Limited, 96
Leonard Street, London, EC2A 4XD, pp4–5, 7; 'Big Fears' by John
Rice reproduced with permission, pp11–12; extract from 'Ghosts: all
in the mind' from BBC News Online at bbc.co.uk, pp19–20; extract
from 'The Apples of the Hesperides' from THE ORCHARD BOOK OF
GREEK MYTHS by Geraldine McCaughrean first published in the UK
by Orchard Books in 1992, a division of The Watts Publishing Group
Limited, 96 Leonard Street, London EC2A 4XD, pp28–29; extract
from 'The Science of Superheroes' from BBC Science & Nature at
bbc.co.uk/sn, p35–36; extract from 'Unidentified Flying Objects' from
BBC Science & Nature at bbc.co.uk/sn, p50–51; extract from ONLY
YOU CAN SAVE MANKIND by Terry Pratchett published by
Doubleday. Used by permission of the Random House Group
Limited, pp56–57; extract from *Alien Life (What's the Big Idea)* by
Jack Challoner (Hodder Children's Books, 1998), p62–63; extract from
Holes by Louis Sachar (Bloomsbury, 2000), p71; 'Should music take
the rap for the increase in gun crime' by Matt Walton from BBC
Collective at bbc.co.uk/collective, © BBC 2002, the BBC's consent
must be obtained for all other uses (contact: Kate Reid, Legal and
Business Affairs Manager 020 75571226), p77–78; 'The Trial of Derek
Drew' from *Heard it in the Playground* by Allan Ahlberg (Viking,
1989) Copyright © Allan Ahlberg, 1989, reproduced with permission
of Penguin Books Ltd., pp83–84; *Let Him Dangle* composed by Elvis
Costello. Published by BMG Music Publishing Ltd. Used by
permission, p85; extract from *Two Weeks with the Queen: Play* by
Mary Morris, based on the novel by Morris Gleitzman (Macmillan
Children's Books, 1994), pp92–94; review 1 from unreel.co.uk ©
Concept Publishing Ltd., pp106–107; review 2 by Rob Andrew (Tiscali
UK Entertainment Editor) from
www.tiscali.co.uk/entertainment/film/reviews/extract, p107; extract
from 'Snake bites' from the Australian Child and Youth Health Agency
website at cyh.com, pp116–117; extract reproduced with permission
from Brazil 5 © 2002 Lonely Planet Publications, p125; 'Bournemouth
in the rain' © Bill Bryson. Extracted from NOTES FROM A SMALL

ISLAND by Bill Bryson, published by Black Swan, a division of
Transworld Publishers. All rights reserved, pp130–131; VSO advert ©
VSO/Kitcatt Nohr Alexander Shaw, p138; Blackpool Sealife Centre
advert reproduced with permission, p139; Wall's Carte D'Or advert
reproduced with kind permission from Unilever ice cream and Frozen
foods UK, p140; extract from 'Is it time to stop worrying' by Lisa
Markwell from *The Independent*, 1 May 2004, pp146–147; extract
from 'Pen pal dangers' from *mizz*, 17 April 2002, pp153–154; extract
from *Boy* by Roald Dahl (Penguin Books, 1992), p162–163; 'It was
long ago' by Eleanor Farjeon from *Blackbird has Spoken* (Macmillan),
pp169–170; extract from 'Ellen MacArthur: back on the high seas'
from BBC News at bbc.co.uk, pp186–187; extract from *Bend it like
Beckham* by Narinder Dhami (Hodder Children's Books, 2002),
p192–193; extract from *Fantastic Sports: Mountain Biking* by Brant
Richards (Aladdin Books, 1998), pp199–200.

Images: AA World Travel Library: p24, 137; Advertising Archive:
pp147, 146, 150; Alamy Ltd: pp17, 77, 152; Alasdair Bright, NB
Illustration: pp 29, 31, 34, 84, 87, 85; Aquarius Collection: pp.49, 70,
71, 73, 74, 109, 112, 180, 193; Ardea: pp120; BBC: p114; Bluegreen:
p191; Buzz Pictures: p199; Courtauld Institute of Art: p181; Culture
Archive: p184; Fogden Photographic Library: p116; Getty Images:
pp12, 14, 18, 41, 50, 104, 153, 155, 200, 202; Idols Licensing and
Publicity: pp78, 159; Jonatronix: pp25, 68, 69; Lonely Planet Images:
p119; Marco Schaaf, NB Illustration: pp58, 60; Mary Evans Picture
Library: pp20, 22, 53, 165; Movie Store Collection Ltd: pp49, 106,
179, 192, 195; PA Photos: pp80, 124, 130, 131, 133, 187, 207;
Popperfoto: p162; Ronald Grant Archive: pp35, 36, 38, 40, 55, 65,
63; RSPCA Photolibrary: p117; Sarah Naylor, NB Illustration: pp4, 6,
8; Stephanie Strickland: pp170, 172; Sue Cunningham Photographic:
pp123, 125, 127

Whilst every effort has been made both to contact the copyright
holders and to give exact credit lines, this has not proved possible in
every case.

Printed and bound by Printing Express, Hong Kong